MAKE IT BY THE BOOK

This edition published by Parragon Books Ltd in 2016 and distributed by

Parragon Inc.
440 Park Avenue South, 13th Floor
New York, NY 10016
www.parragon.com

Copyright © Parragon Books Ltd 2016

Crafts by Rachael Fisher, Kat Roberts, and Kate Woods
Edited by Becky Wilson and Grace Harvey
Designed by Rachael Fisher and Karissa Santos
Stock photography by Shutterstock and iStock
Production by Charlene Vaughan
Designed, produced, and packaged by Rachael Creates

ISBN 978-1-4723-9212-1

Printed in China

MAKE IT BY THE BOOK

Parragon

Bath · New York · Cologne · Melbourne · Delhi
Hong Kong · Shenzhen · Singapore · Amsterdam

CONTENTS

Glitter bug magnets	32
Duvet den tepee	34
Introduction	8
Mon-stir crazy doorstop	36
Tools and materials	10
De-light-ful confetti cups	38
Tips and techniques	12
Twice-as-mice gift boxes	40
Bead-iful bowl	16
Super-stitch tote bag	44
Ro-box bowling	18
Easy-peasy print gift wrap	46
Tape-tastic candies	22
Nifty nail polish flowers	48
Bookcase dollhouse	24
Sweet donut cushions	50
Arm-knitted circle scarf	26
Selfie posing props	54
Star-mâché pencil case	30
Keep-tape family tree	56

Straw-some shapes 60

Ribbon weave diary 88

Pour-in paint vases 62

Phone sock cozy 90

Paper-shaper chain belt 64

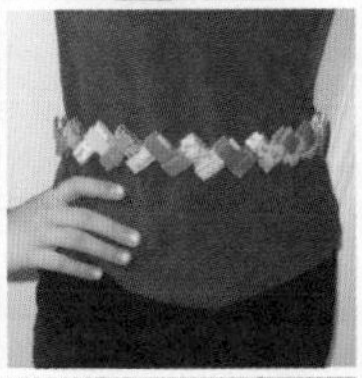

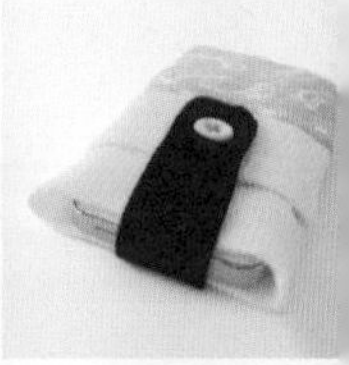

Totally emoji balls 92

Stylish spinners 68

Stick-errific arm cuffs 94

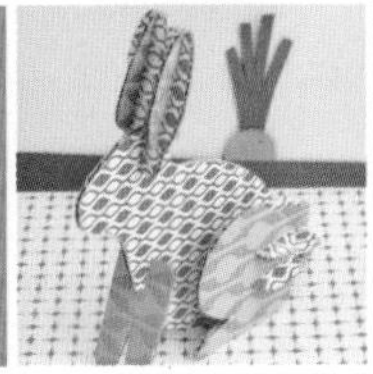

Dino-mite chess game 70

Pigeon picture holders 96

Sew-cute cupcake card 72

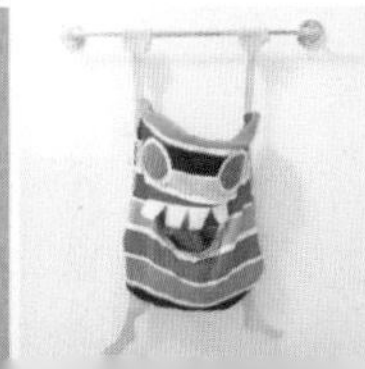

Zip-mouth monsters 100

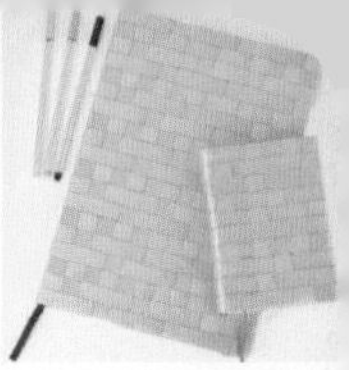

Lava-ly bubbly in a jar 74

Washi tape makeovers 102

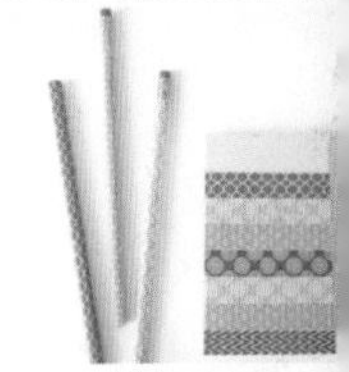

Bunny buddy 76

Cutie fruity felt pouches 104

Pom-pom letter 80

Tissue box clock 106

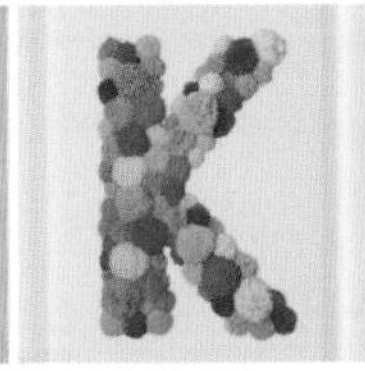

Fant-Aztec lampshade 82

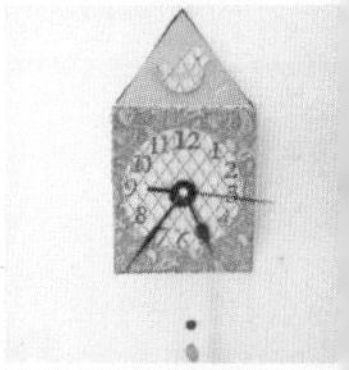

Sewing pin dreamcatcher 110

Laundry bag beastie 84

Seafarin' pet photo booth 112

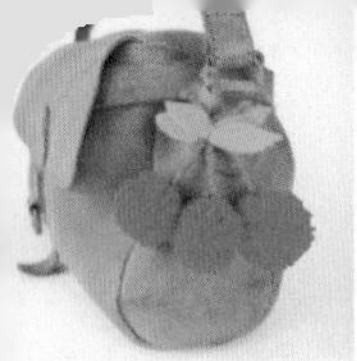

Pom-pom cherry charms 114

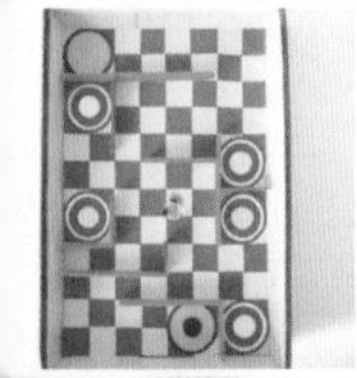

A-maze-ing marble game 116

Bobby pin necklace 120

Rail-life sock ninjas 122

Cool carton money box 126

String-mâché garland 128

Tape-omized cables 'n' cases 130

In-the-frame lampshade 132

Glitter storm photos 134

Ele-box bookends 136

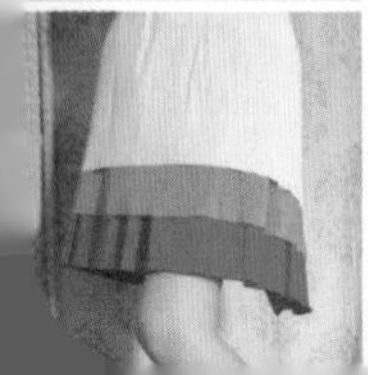

Paper ra-ra skirt 140

Face-the-fox pillow 144

Rain cloud mobile 146

Shrink-tastic keyring 148

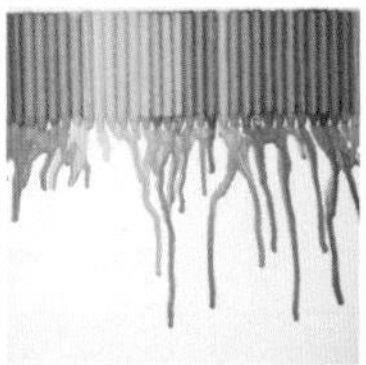

Melted crayon masterpiece 150

Top-dog draft stopper 152

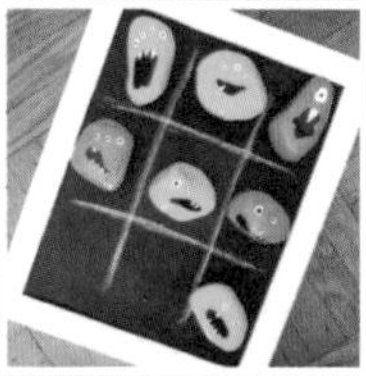

Tic-tac-ohhhh! 156

Pen-chanting patterns 158

Eye spot a peacock 160

Cool cardboard castle 162

Glove-ly octopus 168

Quilling balloon ride 170

Cozy crochet tablet case 172

Super spoon mirror 176

Crane orig-army 178

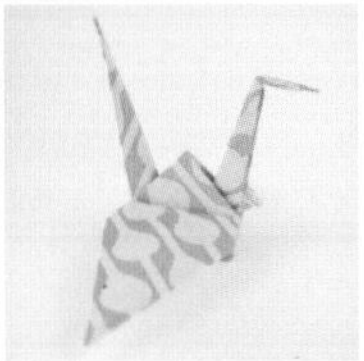

Fabu-mash pineapple print 182

Spotty knotty bag 184

Fairy-tale spoon puppets 186

Theater box 188

Pretty bead suncatcher 190

Comic strip tabletop 192

Fluttering butterflies 194

Pincushion cactus 196

Stamp-imal file box 200

Paper bead bracelet 202

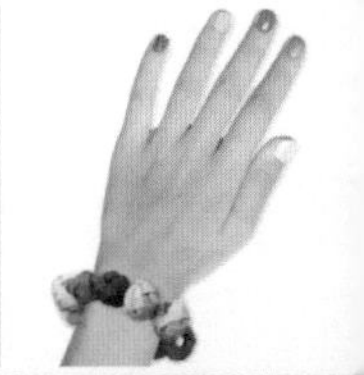

Floor snakes and ladders 204

Giant dice 208

Hula hoop rug 210

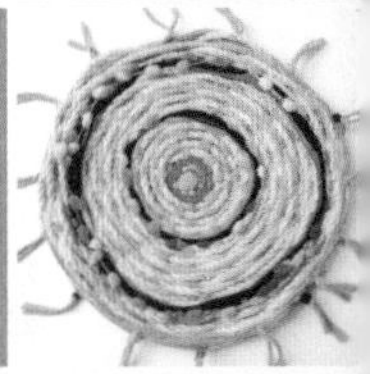

Stitch people 214

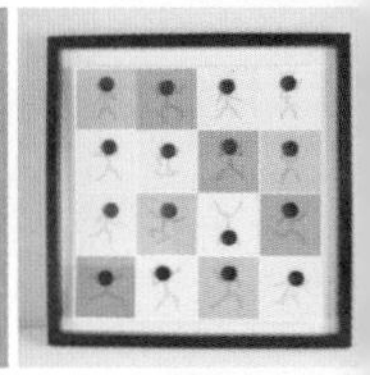

A tubular Advent calendar 216

Neon note monsters 220

Index 222

INTRODUCTION

Get ready to unleash your creativity with over 80 ideas for going craft-crazy!

What's crafting? It's creating, inventing, recycling, and upcycling all rolled into one! It's making something new from something old. It's making something new from something new. It's MAKING something.

Be inspired by the things around you! Turn toilet paper tubes into an Advent calendar, odd socks into coat hook ninjas, and empty cardboard boxes into a full-on castle.

So what are you waiting for? Have a go, experiment, try something new, and get crafting!

TOOLS AND MATERIALS

Arm yourself with some basic craft supplies, so you're ready to get creative whenever you want!

DRAWING, CUTTING, MEASURING, AND MORE!

Pencils, markers, pens, rulers, paintbrushes, scissors, craft knives, and measuring tapes are all essential tools to have around. Some crafts may suggest using a specific tool, but you can always alter the craft if you don't want to spend money on something new.

colored and patterned paper

tracing paper

tissue paper

crepe paper

white paper

cardstock

PAPER

There are many different types of paper, cardstock, and cardboard available, from tissue paper to patterned gift wrap, and sheets of cardstock to cardboard boxes. Stock up on some essentials and have fun making things like origami birds, crepe paper skirts, and even cardboard castles!

FABRICS, FELT, AND FOAM

Most of the projects in this book use lightweight fabrics. Others include canvas fabric—a heavy-duty material perfect for hardwearing crafts. Felt and foam sheets are easy to cut and glue, and felt can even be sewn!

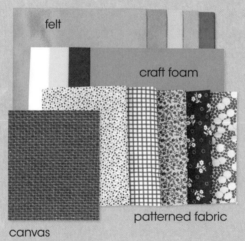

felt

craft foam

patterned fabric

canvas

duct tape

washi tape

masking tape

TAPE

Washi tape comes in lots of colors and patterns, so it's great for decorating and creating big pieces of art. It's also easy to remove if you change your mind! Masking tape is an all-purpose tape, while duct tape is brightly colored and long-lasting.

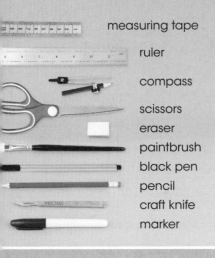

measuring tape
ruler
compass
scissors
eraser
paintbrush
black pen
pencil
craft knife
marker

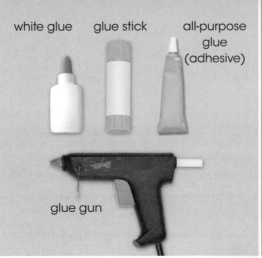

white glue
glue stick
all-purpose glue (adhesive)
glue gun

GLUES

White glue is ideal for most basic crafts, glue sticks are mess-free but mainly used with paper, glue guns are great for cardstock, fabric, plastic, and wood, while all-purpose glues (adhesives) are fab on almost anything!

* Always ask an adult to help when using all-purpose glue and glue guns. Check safety labeling before use.

COLOR

As well as colored pencils, acrylic paints, and poster paints, experiment with other mediums to color your masterpieces. Make a picture from melted crayons, color flowers with nail polish, or decorate a lampshade using highlighter pens. Be brave and get creative!

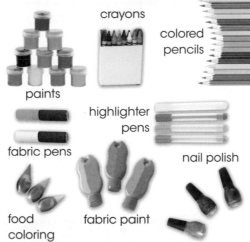

crayons
colored pencils
paints
highlighter pens
fabric pens
nail polish
food coloring
fabric paint

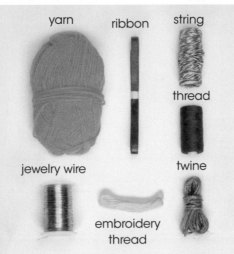

yarn
ribbon
string
thread
jewelry wire
twine
embroidery thread

STRINGS AND THINGS

Thread, yarn, string, twine, and ribbon can be used in many ways. Whether you're stitching material together, knitting something to wear, or hanging up decorations, keep these must-have items close by. If you're mad about jewelry, invest in some jewelry wire (and cutters), too!

HOUSEHOLD STUFF

Everyday objects can easily be upcycled and recycled into fabulous creations, like a glove octopus, a bobby pin necklace, or a juice carton money box. So, before you trash it, think how to treasure it!

socks
juice carton
shoebox
gloves
cake mold
towel
T-shirt
bobby pins
toilet paper tubes

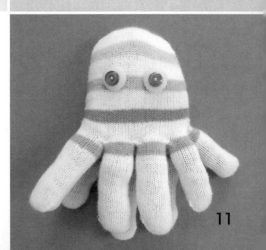

11

TIPS AND TECHNIQUES

Try out different craft-making techniques to gain new skills and take your creations to another level.

MANUFACTURING INSTRUCTIONS

Some crafts may suggest using a specific type of material that also comes with its own instructions. Make sure you read these carefully before you begin. There will be prompts in the "Materials" lists to remind you to ask for help, so look out for the * signs!

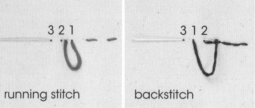

3 2 1
running stitch

3 1 2
backstitch

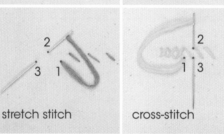

2
3 1
stretch stitch

2
1 3
cross-stitch

SEWING

This book explores a few basic hand-stitching techniques. If you're unsure how to do them, ask an adult to help or to show you video tutorials online. Some crafts also suggest using a sewing machine. Although this is a great timesaver, all of the crafts in this book can be hand-stitched if preferred.

loop 1

1.

loop 1
loop 2

2.

3. feed loop 2 through loop 1

pull tight

4.

KNOTS

These are mainly used to secure a craft or for adding on stitches (as in crochet). Look at these basic knots and practice them so you're familiar with the techniques inside.

The double knot is also known as a square knot.

slip knot   double (square) knot

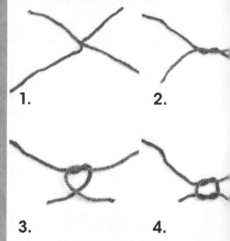

1.   **2.**

3.   **4.**

slip knot—a type of knot used at the start of crocheting

chain—a type of crochet stitch

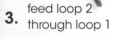

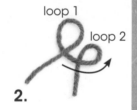

double crochet—a type of crochet stitch

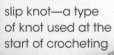

Turn to pages 172–175 to learn more about crochet.

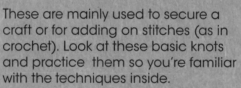

working yarn—the yarn connected to the ball of yarn

tail—the loose end of the yarn

CROCHETING AND KNITTING

We only use a few crochet stitches in this book (shown far left), but if you've never crocheted before, don't worry. Ask an adult to help you or to show you video tutorials online so you can master the basics first. See pages 26–29 for knitting.

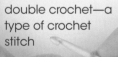

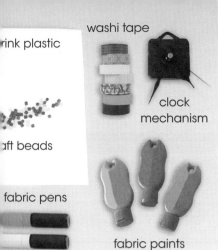

washi tape

rink plastic

clock mechanism

aft beads

fabric pens

fabric paints

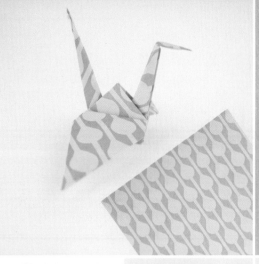

ORIGAMI

Originally associated with Japanese culture, origami is the art of paper folding. If you find some of the steps a bit tricky in this book, ask an adult to help or to show you some online video tutorials. You'll soon be fabulous at folding!

↵

QUILLING

Quilling, or paper filigree, involves rolling, curling, twisting, looping, shaping, and gluing together strips of paper to create a design. Paper coils are curled more quickly and easily with a quilling tool than they are by hand, so it might be worth investing in this special tool if you like quilling. ↳

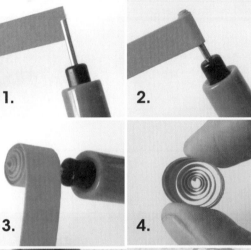

1. **2.** **3.** **4.**

PRINTING

Everyday objects can make great stamping tools, such as kitchen utensils, buttons, bubble wrap, toilet paper tubes, and more. Look around your home and see if you can find anything that could create a perfect print, too.

↵

TOP TIPS

As with anything, practice makes perfect. The more you make, the better you'll get and the faster you'll go! You'll also pick up some top tips that can be used on other crafts, too. Try these handy hints (shown right) in your craft making.*

* Ask an adult for help! ↳

To make a central hole in a piece of cardstock (or paper), place a blob of adhesive putty at the back and wiggle a pencil through into the putty.

To help cardstock bend more easily, lightly score it first using scissors (or a craft knife) and a metal ruler. 13

BEAD-IFUL BOWL

EASY BEAD-Y!

paper table napkin   oven-proof bowl

MATERIALS →

cooking oil

small, fusible plastic beads*

How do itty bitty beads keep all your odds and ends safe? Just melt them together to make a fabulous bead bowl. Now that's crafty!

* Beads must be suitable for craft making and use with an iron or oven!

1. Preheat the oven to 400°F.* Then pour a few drops of oil into the bowl. This will help the beads to stick to the sides in step 3.

* Ask an adult to do this!

2. Use a paper napkin to spread the oil evenly around the bowl. Make sure you cover the whole area, otherwise the beads might not stay in place.

3. Press the beads against the insides of the bowl to form a single layer all around. Create a pretty pattern by alternating the colors in each row!

4. Place the bowl on a baking tray and put it in the oven for 10 minutes.* Keep an eye on the beads, as they may take less or more time to melt together.

* Ask an adult to do this for you.

5. When all the beads have melted, take the bowl out of the oven and leave to cool for 15 minutes.

6. Finally, carefully tip the melted beads out of the bowl. They should now be a bowl shape, too!

17

Create a fab robot bowling game. Turn empty boxes into dangerous droids, then line 'em up and knock 'em down. The player who strikes the most robots with the ball is the winner!

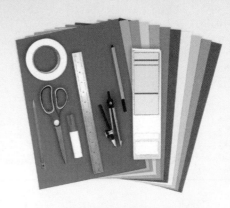

MATERIALS

tall, narrow, empty food boxes x 10, colored paper, pencil, ruler, tape, scissors, glue stick, compass, black pen, ball

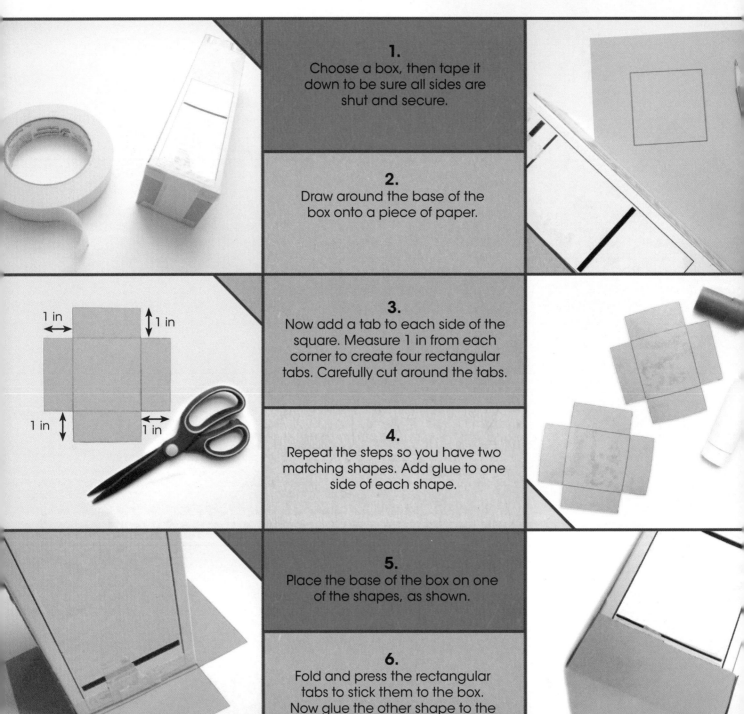

1.
Choose a box, then tape it down to be sure all sides are shut and secure.

2.
Draw around the base of the box onto a piece of paper.

3.
Now add a tab to each side of the square. Measure 1 in from each corner to create four rectangular tabs. Carefully cut around the tabs.

1 in   1 in

1 in   1 in

4.
Repeat the steps so you have two matching shapes. Add glue to one side of each shape.

5.
Place the base of the box on one of the shapes, as shown.

6.
Fold and press the rectangular tabs to stick them to the box. Now glue the other shape to the top of the box.

7.
When the top and base of the box are covered with paper, use your ruler to measure the length of the box.

8.
Cut out a piece of paper the same length as the box, making sure it is wide enough to wrap around all four sides. Add 1 in extra to the width to make a tab.

length of box

side 1 | side 2 | side 3 | side 4 | tab

width of box | 1 in

9.
Glue the paper and wrap it around the box, completely covering any original packaging design.

10.
Repeat the previous steps using the rest of your empty boxes and colored paper to make ten "pins."

11.
Using your ruler, compass, and pencil, draw different-sized rectangles, circles, and semicircles on the colored paper to make the heads, arms, bodies, and legs of the robots.

12.
Now cut out all the pieces.

13.
Create each robot character with the cut-out pieces of paper. Glue them to one side of a box, then draw the face, buttons, and dials with black pen.

14.
Repeat step 13 for all the other boxes and then you are ready to play

RO-BOX BOWLING!

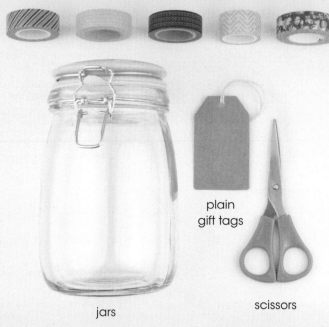

patterned washi tape

plain gift tags

jars

scissors

MATERIALS

Originating in Japan, washi tape is a special kind of tape that's colorful, multi-patterned, and easy to use. It's great for upcycling everyday items, like old jars. Try this super-simple craft and make some sweet gifts for friends and family!

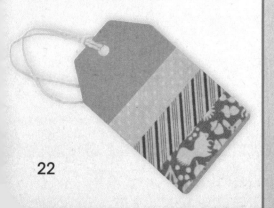

1. Thoroughly clean out the jars before you start.*

2. Choose the washi tape patterns, then stick the tape on the jars. Experiment with vertical, horizontal, or diagonal designs. Cover the jars with tape or leave an area clear to reveal the tasty treats inside.

3. When you've finished, fill the jars with wrapped candies.

4. Decorate the gift tags to match each jar's unique design, then tie them on!

* Ask an adult to clean the jars in a dishwasher or with hot water and dishwashing liquid.

TAPE-TASTIC CANDIES

SHOW ME THE CANDIES!

IT'S A WRAP!

BOOKCASE DOLLHOUSE

MAKE A SHELF
A HOME!

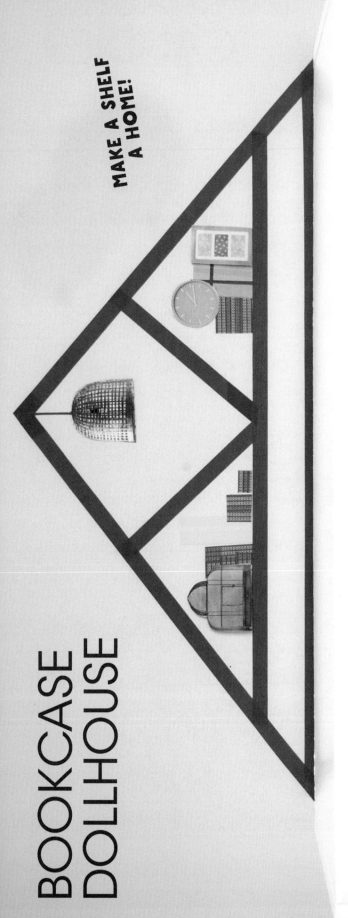

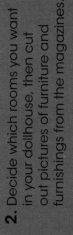

3. Now arrange the pictures in each room and glue them inside. Finish off each room with some doll's furniture and dolls (if you have them).

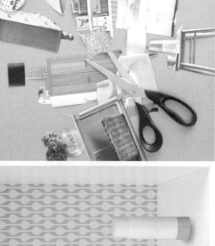

2. Decide which rooms you want in your dollhouse, then cut out pictures of furniture and furnishings from the magazines.

1. Cut out pieces of patterned paper, the same size as the back of each shelf in your bookcase, for the wallpaper. Then glue them in place.

MATERIALS

old bookcase, home and furniture magazines, patterned paper, scissors, glue stick

ARM-KNITTED CIRCLE SCARF

WONDERFULLY WOOLLY!

MATERIALS
balls of yarn x 4,
large needle

1.
Take a strand from each ball of yarn and line up the ends, as shown.

2.
Keeping hold of the yarn, measure out six arm's-lengths of yarn.

3.
Tie a slip knot near the end, leaving the six arm's lengths as a tail. Make sure you keep the four strands of yarn grouped together.

4.
Slide the knot onto your right wrist.

tail

working yarn

5.
In your left hand, hold the four strands of working yarn (the yarn still attached to the ball), then loop them around your thumb and across your palm. Hold the end of the yarn, or the tail, between two fingers, as shown.

working yarn

tail

6.
Slide your right hand under the working yarn (stretched taut by your thumb), then grab the tail (being held by your fingers).

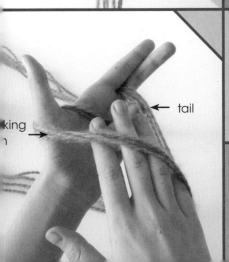

king
n

tail

7.
Pull the tail through the loop that you have just created, but not all the way.

27

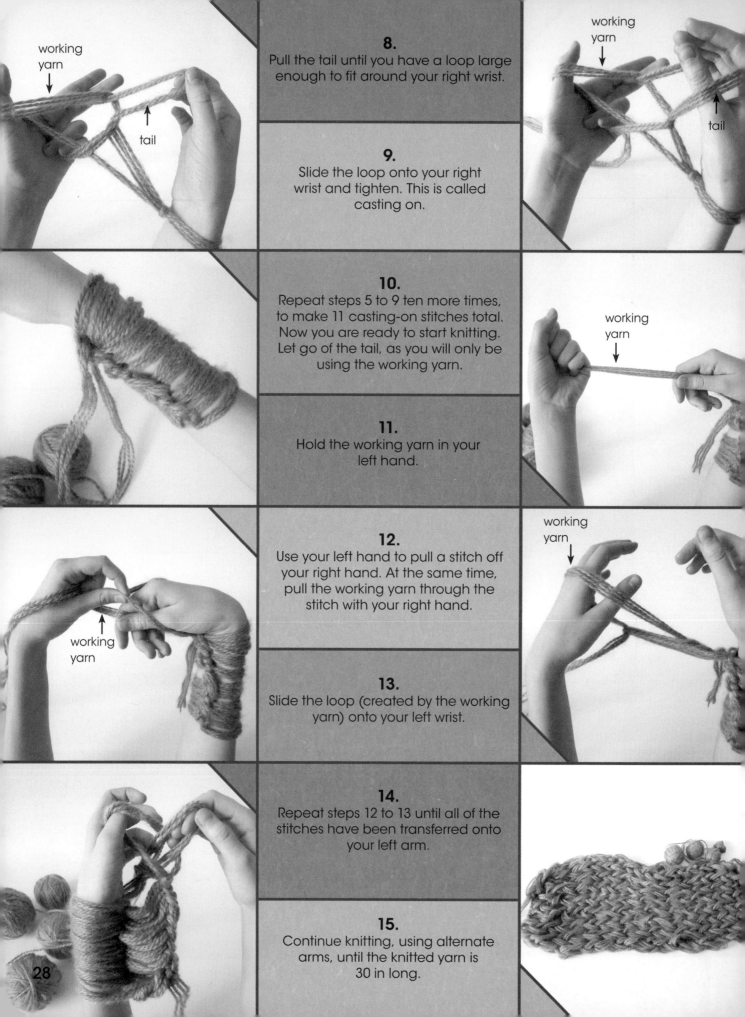

working yarn

tail

8.
Pull the tail until you have a loop large enough to fit around your right wrist.

working yarn

tail

9.
Slide the loop onto your right wrist and tighten. This is called casting on.

10.
Repeat steps 5 to 9 ten more times, to make 11 casting-on stitches total. Now you are ready to start knitting. Let go of the tail, as you will only be using the working yarn.

working yarn

11.
Hold the working yarn in your left hand.

12.
Use your left hand to pull a stitch off your right hand. At the same time, pull the working yarn through the stitch with your right hand.

working yarn

working yarn

13.
Slide the loop (created by the working yarn) onto your left wrist.

14.
Repeat steps 12 to 13 until all of the stitches have been transferred onto your left arm.

15.
Continue knitting, using alternate arms, until the knitted yarn is 30 in long.

16.
Now you're ready to cast off. First, knit two more stitches on your right arm.

17.
With your left hand, pull the first stitch on your right arm over the second stitch, then slide the stitch off your right hand, casting it off. Now pull the yarn tight.

second stitch

first stitch

18.
Knit another stitch on your right arm. Again, pull the first stitch over the second, then slide it off your right hand. Tighten the yarn. Continue until you have completely cast off all the stitches.

19.
Cut the working yarn one arm's length from your last stitch, creating a tail. To prevent the knitting from undoing, pull the tail through the last stitch and tighten.

20.
Thread all four strands of the tail through the eye of a large needle. Fold the knitting in half, lining up the ends, as shown.

21.
Stitch the ends of the scarf together using the needle and tail.

22.
Now split the four tails into two, and tie them together twice to form a double knot (see page 12 to find out how to do this).

23.
Hide the remaining bit of tail by weaving it through the knitting with your needle, and you're done!

long balloon, paper (11 in x 17 in), pin, adhesive putty, paintbrush, bowl of confetti stars, bowl of ¾ white glue and ¼ water mix (as shown)

1.

Blow up the balloon and tie a knot in the end. Place two balls of adhesive putty on each end of the balloon, then place it on the paper. This will stop the balloon from moving.

2.

Now brush the glue mixture evenly over the entire top half of the balloon.

3.

Sprinkle the confetti stars over the balloon, covering as much of the glue area as possible. Leave to dry.

4.

Shake the balloon until all the loose confetti falls onto the paper. Remove the adhesive putty from the paper, then pour the loose confetti back into the bowl.

5.

Repeat steps 1 to 4 three more times, until the top of the balloon is covered with a thin layer of confetti stars.

6.

Finally, paint the confetti with a layer of the glue mixture and leave to dry.

7.

Turn the balloon over, then pop it with a pin. Remove the balloon. Cut around the jagged edge so that it is straight, and fill with pencils!

GIVE YOUR
STATIONERY
A STARRING
ROLE!

STAR-MÂCHÉ PENCIL CASE

GLITTER BUG MAGNETS

CAN I BUG YOU? PLEEEASE?

MATERIALS

white glue

glitter nail polish

clear glass stones

self-adhesive flexible foam magnets

googly eyes

Bug yourself with lists, notes, mementos, or reminders with these fab forget-me-not fridge magnets. Make them super-sparkly to stand out on your fridge!

1. Paint the back of a clear stone with some glitter nail polish. Leave to dry.

2. Add a few more coats of polish to give an even color. Allow time to dry between each coat.

3. Read the instructions for the sticky magnet, then attach it to the back of the stone.

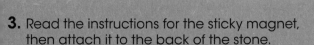

4. Glue googly eyes to the front of the stone. Create more glitter bugs, then place them on the fridge!

MATERIALS

⌐→

double duvet cover,
bamboo canes x 5
(each 70 in long),
bamboo canes x 4
(each 20 in long),
twine, scissors

12 in

1. Wrap some twine around the five longer canes (12 in down from the top of the canes). Tie the twine in a double knot, then cut it off.

2. Open out two of the canes from the bottom end. Place a shorter length of bamboo between them, then tie together with more twine, as shown, securing with double knots.

3. Repeat step 2 until all the shorter lengths of cane have been tied between the longer lengths, as shown.

a

b

4. Stand the frame up, arranging the canes into a tepee shape.

5. (a) Tie one corner of the duvet cover around the top of the tepee with a knot. (b) Repeat this step with the adjacent duvet cover corner.

6. Tie one remaining duvet cover corner around the bottom of each front bamboo cane to finish!

LET'S GO CAMPING!

DUVET
DEN
TEPEE

35

MON-STIR CRAZY DOORSTOP

OUCH!

MATERIALS

purple canvas fabric, colored felt (black, white, yellow, and pink), scissors, ruler, pencil, needle, thread, dried lentils

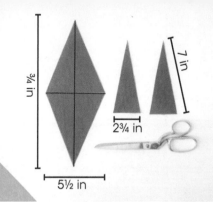

1.
Draw a cross 13 in long x 5½ in wide onto the back of the canvas fabric. Draw lines to join the points to make a diamond. Now draw two triangles, 7 in along each side and 2¾ in at each base. Cut them out.

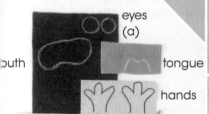

eyes (a)

mouth

tongue

hands

2.
Sketch the eyes, mouth, tongue, and hands onto the pieces of felt, as shown. Carefully cut these out, too.

3.
Backstitch the black circles (a) onto the white ones (b) (for eyes), and the pink tongue in the black mouth. Turn the canvas fabric over to the front and stitch the eyes and mouth in the top half of the diamond.

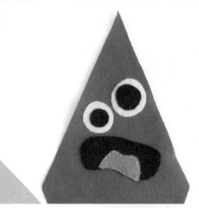

4.
Place one yellow hand in the top half of the diamond. Now place the long side of a purple triangle on top, lining it up along the edge of the diamond. Backstitch along the edge so the hand is sandwiched between the two purple layers.

5.
Repeat step 4 on the other side of the diamond.

6.
Fold the bottom half of the diamond upward so that the tips touch and the monster's face is on the inside.

7.
Now sew each open edge of the triangles to each open edge of the diamond, leaving a gap at the top.

8.
Turn the monster inside out, through the gap at the top, so its face is on the outside again. Fill your monster doorstop with dried lentils.

9.
Finish by folding in the top edges and sewing up the opening with a running stitch.

DE-LIGHT-FUL CONFETTI CUPS

MATERIALS

battery-powered string lights, round tissue paper confetti, paper cups, pencil, brush, white glue, water

1.

Mix together ⅔ white glue with ⅓ water in a bowl. Brush a small amount of the mixture (about the size of a confetti piece) onto a cup.

2.

Stick a single piece of confetti onto the glue area, as shown.

FABULOUS FOR PARTIES!

3.
Repeat steps 1 and 2, adding more confetti pieces to the cup. Try overlapping some.

4.
Turn the cup upside down and, using a sharp pencil, pierce a small hole in the base of the cup.

5.
Thread one light through the hole in the cup. Repeat steps 1 to 4 until you have enough cups for all the lights.

TWICE-AS-MICE GIFT BOXES

SQUEAK! SQUEAK!

WHAT A MICE IDEA!

MATERIALS

patterned paper x 4
(12 in x 12 in x 2, 6 in x 6 in x 2),
pink paper, ruler, scissors, pencil,
glue stick, black pen

1.
Use a 12 in x 12 in piece of paper to create the base of your large box.

2.
Fold the paper in half, then unfold it.

3.
Fold the paper in half the other way, and unfold.

4.
Turn the paper over onto the other side. Fold one corner up into the middle of the crease lines created in steps 2 and 3.

5.
Repeat step 4 until all four corners have been folded into the center.

6.
Using your ruler, fold the right-hand side toward the center (2½ in in from the edge), then unfold.

2½ in

7.
Repeat step 6 for the left-hand, bottom, and top sides.

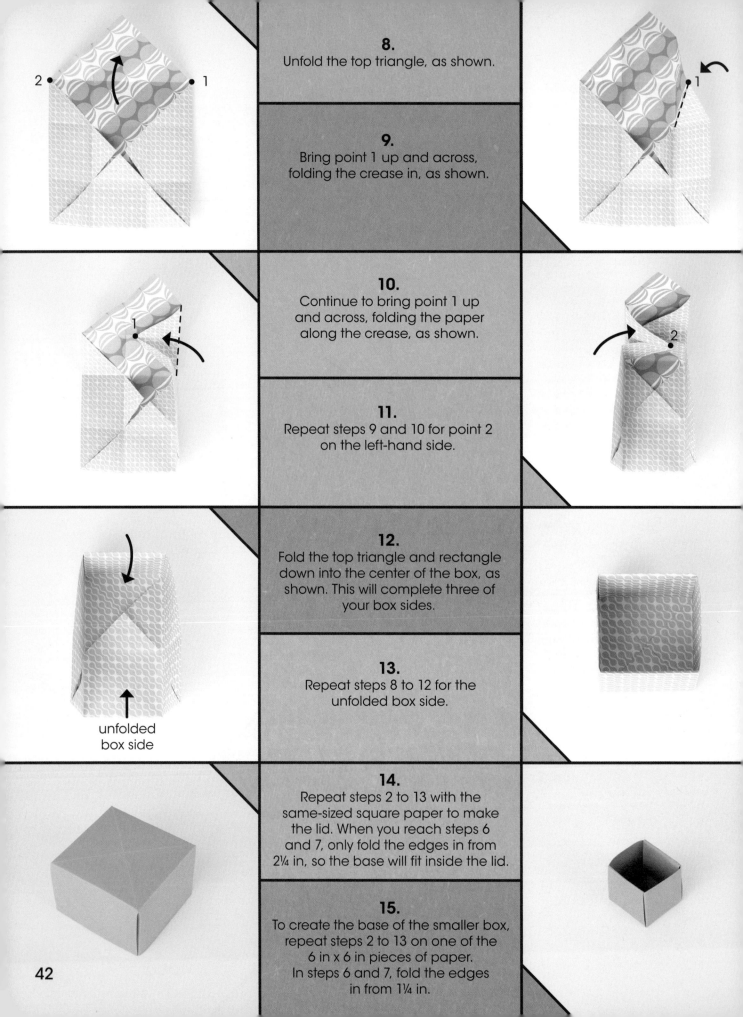

8.
Unfold the top triangle, as shown.

9.
Bring point 1 up and across, folding the crease in, as shown.

10.
Continue to bring point 1 up and across, folding the paper along the crease, as shown.

11.
Repeat steps 9 and 10 for point 2 on the left-hand side.

12.
Fold the top triangle and rectangle down into the center of the box, as shown. This will complete three of your box sides.

13.
Repeat steps 8 to 12 for the unfolded box side.

14.
Repeat steps 2 to 13 with the same-sized square paper to make the lid. When you reach steps 6 and 7, only fold the edges in from 2¼ in, so the base will fit inside the lid.

15.
To create the base of the smaller box, repeat steps 2 to 13 on one of the 6 in x 6 in pieces of paper. In steps 6 and 7, fold the edges in from 1¼ in.

2

1

1

1

2

unfolded box side

16.
Repeat steps 2 to 13 with the same-sized paper to make the lid of the small box. In steps 6 and 7, only fold the edges in from 1 in.

17.
To turn your boxes into mice, draw two tails and two triangular noses on the pink paper. Use the cap of the glue stick to create four circular ears. Add a rectangular tab to each ear.

18.
Carefully cut out all the pieces.

19.
Snip a slot in each of the rectangular tabs, as shown. These will help stick the ears to the boxes in step 21.

20.
Turn the lid of the large box over and glue one of the tails Inside the inner edge. Gently bend the tail a little so it sticks out of the lid.

21.
Glue a nose in the middle of the lid on the opposite side of the tail. Then dab some glue on an ear tab. Stick one side of the slot on the top of the lid, and the other down its side. Repeat with the other ear.

22.
Finish off the large box by drawing some whiskers, eyes, and a mouth with the black pen.

23.
Repeat steps 20 to 22 on the small box to finish. Squeak!

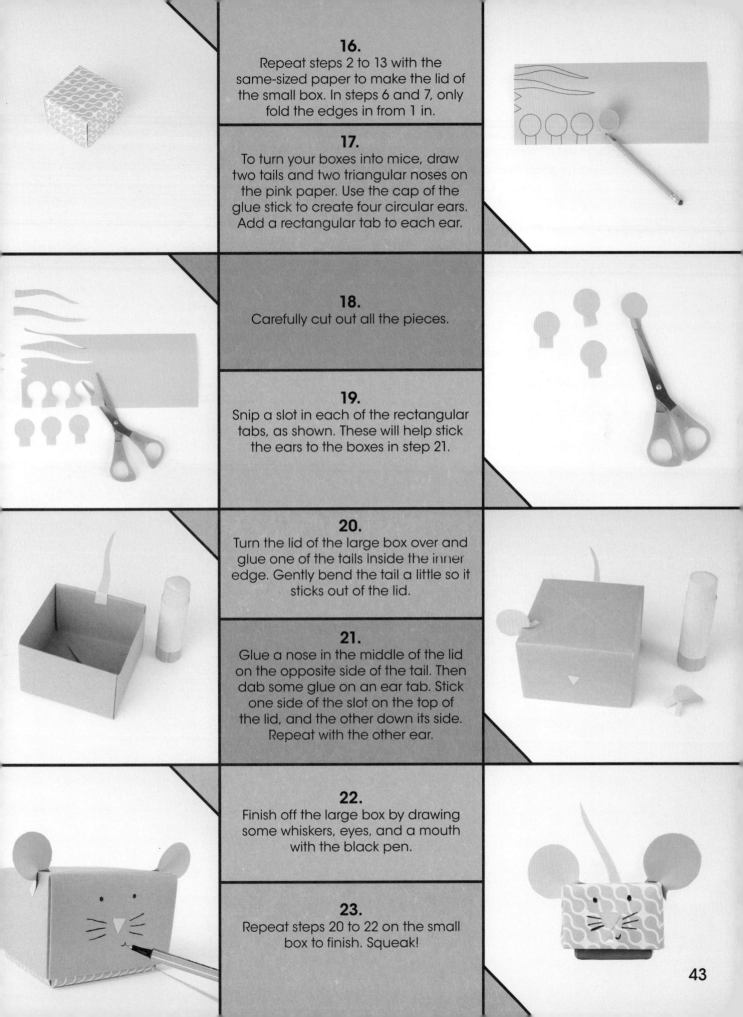

43

MATERIALS
plain tote bag, blue and yellow embroidery thread, needle, ruler, pencil, scissors

1.
With your pencil and ruler, lightly draw a grid across the front of the tote bag. Space the vertical lines 1 in apart, and the horizontal lines ½ in apart.

2.
Start from the top left corner and place four dots where one horizontal line meets a vertical line. Draw the dots on the lines, evenly spaced around the cross. Continue across the bag in a similar pattern as shown.

3.
First, sew on some yellow crosses. Start from inside the bag, feeding the needle through a dot at the bottom of a cross and over into the dot opposite.

4.
Now feed the needle through the dot at the side, and over into the dot opposite. Pull the thread tightly to form a cross.

5.
Tie the thread ends together in a double knot on the inside of the bag and trim with your scissors. Repeat steps 3 and 4 in a few different places on the bag.

6.
For the blue stitches, start from the bottom left inside the bag, feeding the needle through a dot at the bottom of the cross, and over into the dot opposite. Then repeat for the cross above, continuing to form vertical blue lines up and down the bag.

7.
Now work your way back across the bag, sewing horizontal blue lines through the vertical lines to finish. Tie a double knot at the end!

SUPER-STITCH TOTE BAG

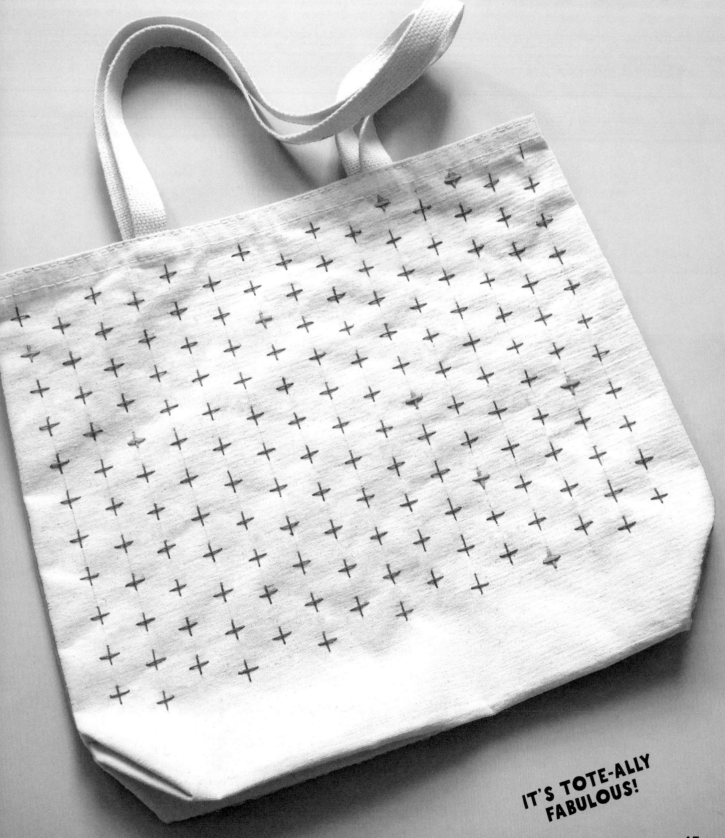

IT'S TOTE-ALLY FABULOUS!

EASY-PEASY PRINT GIFT WRAP

Who needs to buy wrapping paper when you can make your own? From buttons to bubble wrap, and paintbrushes to potatoes, be inspired to create fabulous prints using everyday objects found around the home.

Patterned buttons make fab stampers. Glue them to something sturdy (like cork stoppers) to prevent your finger from getting messy!

Have fun with easy-peasy potato prints. Try hearts, stars, and smiley faces, or opt for a simple semicircle pattern!

For instant printing, use the end of a toilet paper tube and create some seriously cool circles!

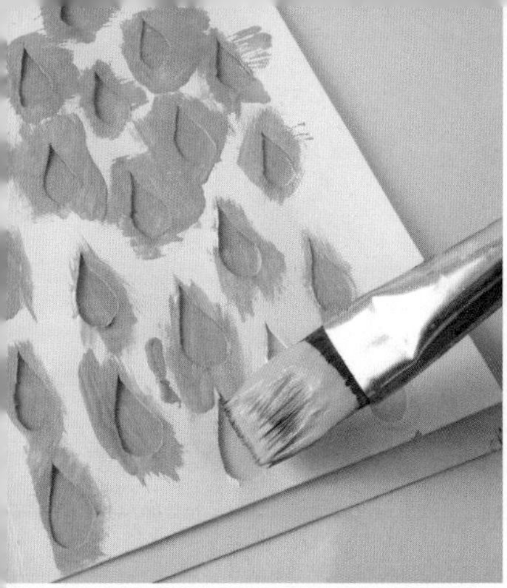

Stencils make great patterns, like this raindrop effect. Just cut out your design from cardstock, then paint over the top!

Raid your pencil case and create a polka-dot pattern with the end of a pencil (or pen) dipped in an ink pad.

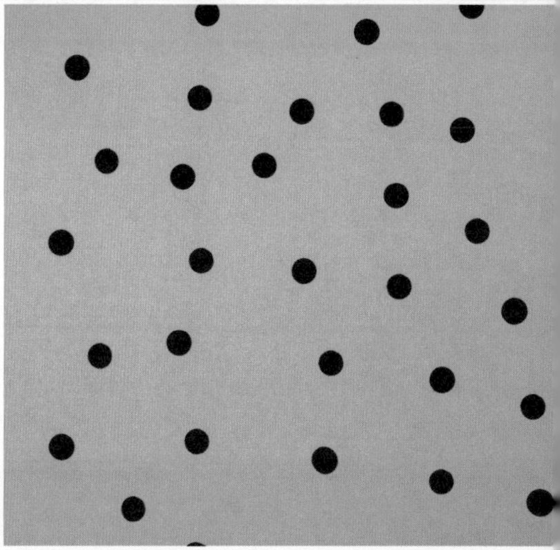

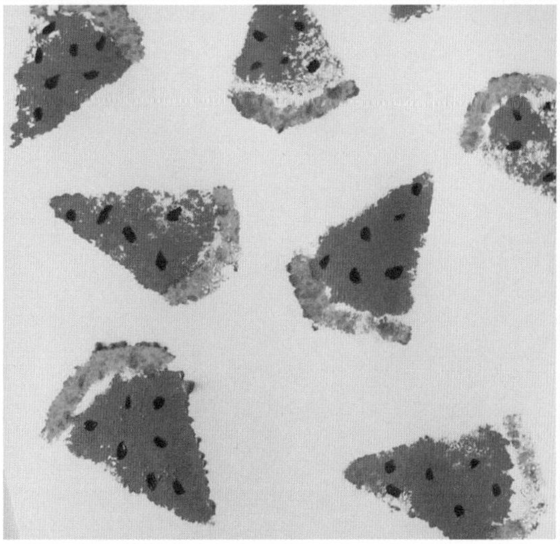

For a more detailed print, stamp two colors at the same time from a piece of shaped sponge. Once it dries, add any finer details (like the seeds in this watermelon) with more paint and a brush!

Brush poster paint over bubble wrap for a bright and bubbly design!

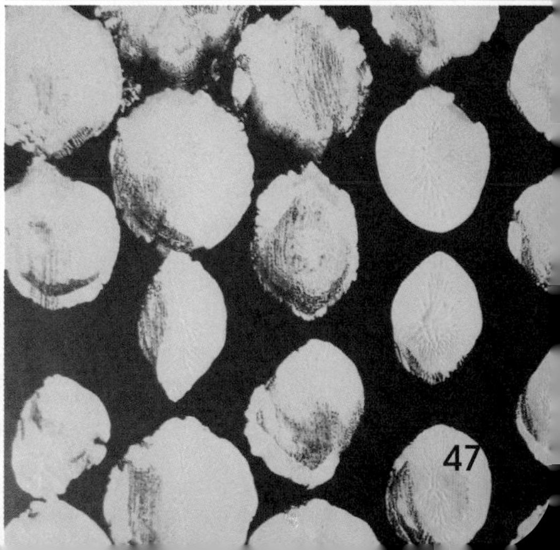

BUZZ!

WHAT
BEE-UTIFUL
FLOWERS!

NIFTY
NAIL
POLISH
FLOWERS

MATERIALS

colored nail polish, jewelry wire,
jewelry pliers (with cutter), thin metal rod or
wooden skewer, jar, pen

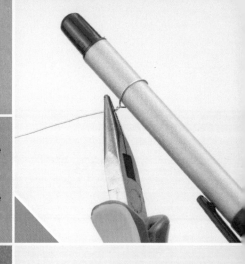

1.

Cut the jewelry wire to 16 in long, then bend the middle part of the wire around the barrel of a pen with the pliers. Now rotate the pen so that the wire becomes twisted together beneath the loop on the pen. Slide the wire loop off the pen.

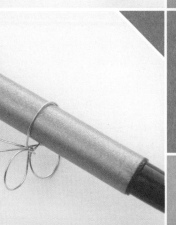

2.

Next, wrap one end of the wire around the pen to create another loop next to the first one. Feed the same end of the wire through the center of the first loop, to join them together. Then repeat to create a third loop with the other end of the wire.

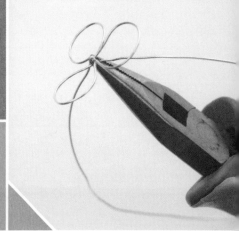

3.

As the loops start to look like flower petals, twist both ends of the wire near the center, to tie them all together.

4.

Repeat steps 2 and 3 to form two more petals. You may need to move the position of the first three petals to make room.

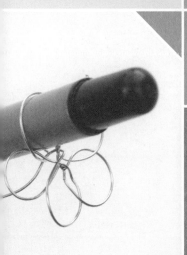

5.

Now place the flower on the metal rod or wooden skewer, as shown. Take one end of the wire and wrap it tightly around the skewer. Do the same with the other end of the wire, but twist it around the skewer in the opposite direction.

6.

To create a leaf, cut the wire to 4 in long, then bend the middle around the pen with the pliers. Rotate the pen so that the wire twists together beneath the loop on the pen. Slide the loop off the pen, then pinch it into a leaf shape. Create more leaves in the same way!

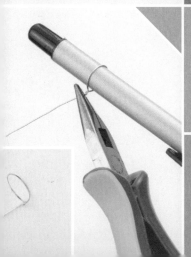

7.

Pour the nail polish into a jar. Dip the petals and leaves into the polish until fully coated. Leave to dry between each coat. Finally, twist the leaves around the skewers and place your flowers in a vase or bottle to finish.

YUM YUM!

NAUGHTY BUT N-ICE!

SWEET DONUT CUSHIONS

MATERIALS

felt (beige, pink, dark brown, and white),
paper plate x 2, pencil, scissors, needle, thread,
embroidery thread (yellow, pink, blue, and green),
toy stuffing

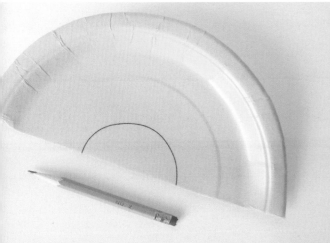

1. First fold a paper plate in half. Then draw a
semicircle inside it, as shown.

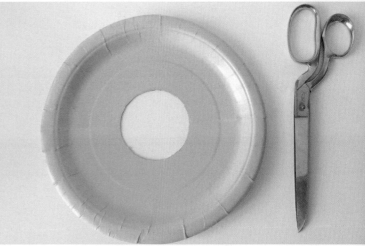

2. Carefully cut along the line and unfold
the plate to reveal a hole in the middle.

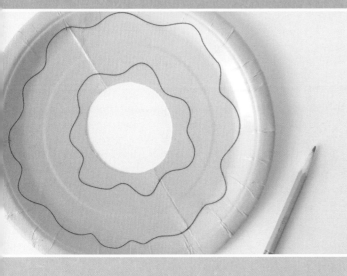

3. Repeat steps 1 and 2 on another paper plate.
Then draw two squiggly circles, as shown.

4. Cut along each line to make a ring. These are
now the templates for your donut cushions.

51

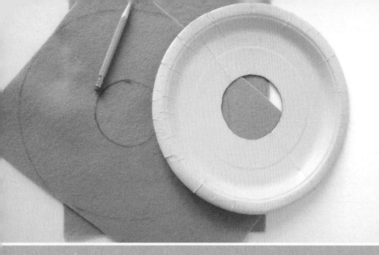

5. For the main donut shape, draw around the circular plate onto two pieces of beige felt.

6. Trace the squiggly shape onto one of the other felt colors. This will be the frosting.

7. Carefully cut out all of the pieces, as shown.

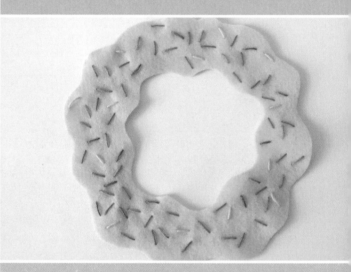

8. Create the look of sprinkles by sewing large stitches of different colors all over the felt frosting.

9. Now sew the felt frosting onto one of the beige circles. Stitch all around both edges of the frosting.

10. Keep the other beige circle plain (as this will be the bottom of the donut ring).

52

11. Pin the two beige rings together, with the frosting on the inside.

12. Stitch the circles together, going all around the outer edges.

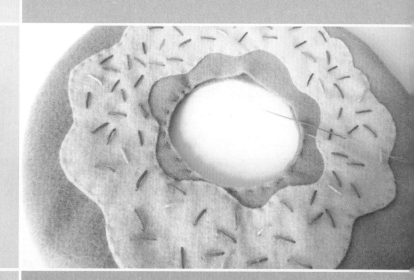

13. Turn out the donut so the frosting is now on the outside, as shown.

14. Stitch ¾ of the way around the inner edges of the rings, leaving an opening for the stuffing.

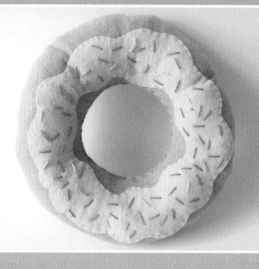

15. Feed the stuffing through the hole until the donut shape is completely full.

16. Sew the opening up to finish. Make more donut ring cushions with different-colored felt frosting. Delicious!

53

SELFIE POSING PROPS

MATERIALS
colored cardstock, wooden skewers, pencil, scissors, glue gun*

*Ask an adult to use the glue gun in step 3!

1. Draw or trace some fun mustaches, beards, hats, glasses, ties, or whatever you wish onto th back of different pieces of colored cardstock.

2. Carefully cut out all of the shapes.

3. Dab some glue in one corner of each piece with the glue gun.*

   *Ask an adult to do th

4. Press a skewer firmly onto the glue.

GRAB A PROP AND STRIKE A POSE!

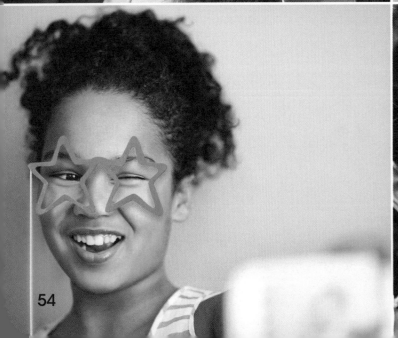

MY FAMILY

MY SISTER AND ME

DAD

MOM AND ME

Show off fabulous family photos with this washi tape family tree. Create new branches, add more pictures, and update any old ones as you go!*

MATERIALS

brown, green (a few shades and patterns), yellow, orange, and red rolls of washi tape, scissors

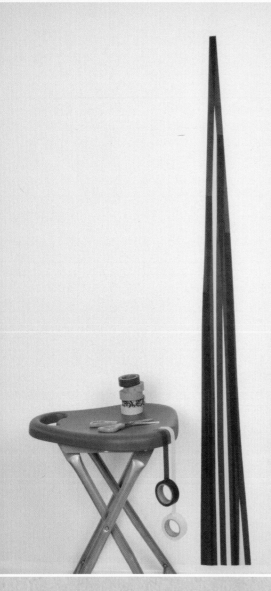

1. Clean a big wall space area, then run strips of brown and yellow washi tape from the floor upward to make the tree trunk (60 in long). The trunk should be wider at the bottom and taper to a point at the top.

2. For the branches, run different lengths of tape at angles from the trunk, as shown. Again, make the branches wider near the trunk and narrower at the tip. Add smaller lengths of brown tape for the twigs.

3. To make a leaf shape, first cut out some green tape (7 in long) for the stem, then stick it on the wall near the branches. Now add four smaller lengths of tape for the veins and place on the stem, as shown.

4. Use another shade of green for the outer edges of the leaf. Tape four strips around the stem and the veins to form a diamond. Repeat steps 3 and 4 to make more leaves in different shades and colors.

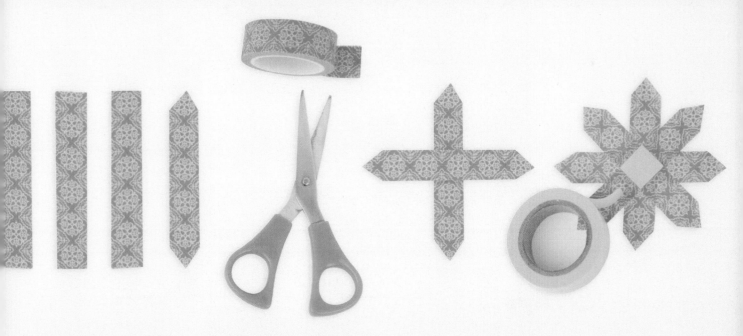

5. To make each flower, first cut four strips of orange washi tape for the petals. Keep the strips the same length (3 in each), then snip the ends to form triangular tips.

6. Stick one orange strip on the wall, then add another on top to form a cross. Add the other two strips, as shown, and cut out a small yellow square for the middle of the flower. Repeat steps 5 and 6 to make more flowers. Now tape your photos to the wall!

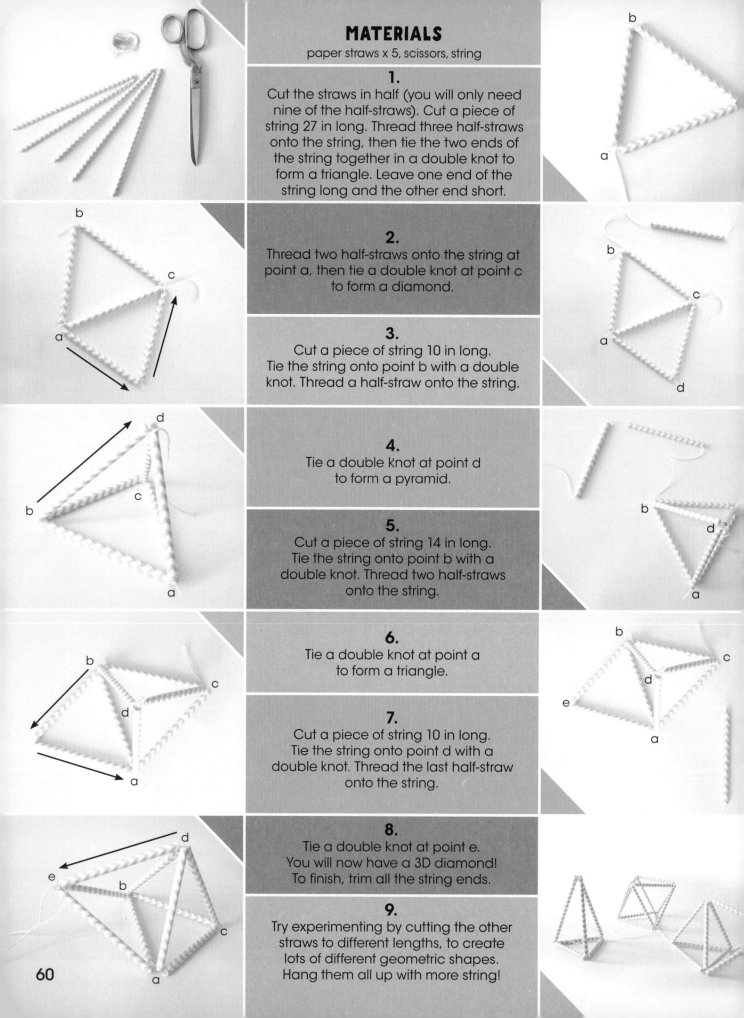

MATERIALS
paper straws x 5, scissors, string

1.
Cut the straws in half (you will only need nine of the half-straws). Cut a piece of string 27 in long. Thread three half-straws onto the string, then tie the two ends of the string together in a double knot to form a triangle. Leave one end of the string long and the other end short.

2.
Thread two half-straws onto the string at point a, then tie a double knot at point c to form a diamond.

3.
Cut a piece of string 10 in long. Tie the string onto point b with a double knot. Thread a half-straw onto the string.

4.
Tie a double knot at point d to form a pyramid.

5.
Cut a piece of string 14 in long. Tie the string onto point b with a double knot. Thread two half-straws onto the string.

6.
Tie a double knot at point a to form a triangle.

7.
Cut a piece of string 10 in long. Tie the string onto point d with a double knot. Thread the last half-straw onto the string.

8.
Tie a double knot at point e. You will now have a 3D diamond! To finish, trim all the string ends.

9.
Try experimenting by cutting the other straws to different lengths, to create lots of different geometric shapes. Hang them all up with more string!

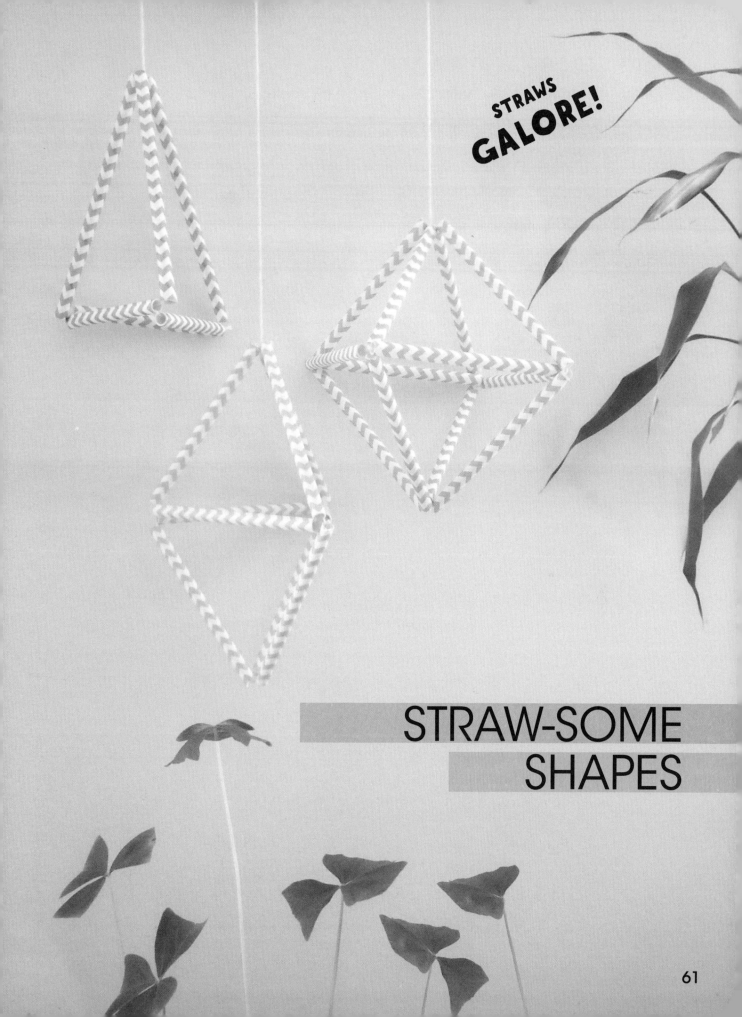

STRAWS
GALORE!

STRAW-SOME
SHAPES

Upcycle an old jar into a brightly colored vase with this easy-peasy craft. Try adding more amazing creations to your budding collection with different-shaped jars (or bottles) and colors.

poster paints
glass jar (or bottle)
funnel

MATERIALS

1.
Place the funnel on the top of a clean, dry jar (or bottle).*

* Ask an adult to clean the jar in a dishwasher or with hot water and dishwashing liquid.

2.
Pour some poster paint into the bottom of the jar through the funnel.

3.
Tip the jar on its side and let the paint flow down the side of the jar. Keep turning the jar around for an even coat of paint along the sides.

4.
Continue to rotate the sides of the jar until the paint is right up to the rim of the jar. Then leave to dry.

GO COLOR CRAZY!

POUR-IN PAINT VASES

PAPER-SHAPER CHAIN BELT

A FABULOUS WAIST OF PAPER!

MATERIALS

patterned paper x 15,
self-adhesive hook-and-loop
fastener (6 in long),
binder clips x 2,
white glue,
scissors

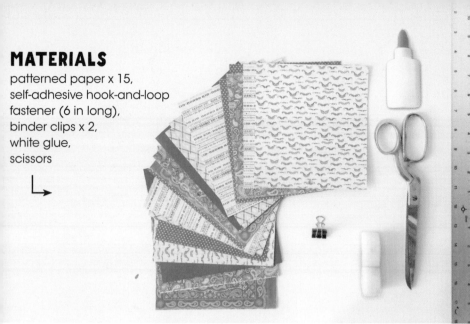

Turn patterned paper into a beautiful belt! Fold and link lots of pieces of paper together to make your very own paper-trail accessory.

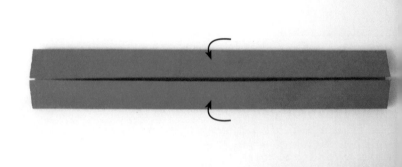

1. First measure your waist, then add an extra 4½ in. This will be the length of your paper chain. Now cut the paper into lots of strips, each one measuring 2 in x 6 in.

2. First, fold each strip in half lengthwise to mark the center. Unfold and then fold each strip lengthwise twice, bringing each edge toward the center.

3. Now fold along the center line, so the folded edges from step 2 are on the inside.

4. Now fold the strip in half widthwise to mark the center. Unfold and then fold each strip widthwise twice, bringing each edge toward the center.

65

5. Then fold along the center line, so the folded edges from step 4 are on the inside.

6. Pinch the two ends together.

7. Repeat steps 1 to 6 until you have lots of folded pieces. Now you're ready to get connecting.

8. Insert the ends of one piece though the folds of another.

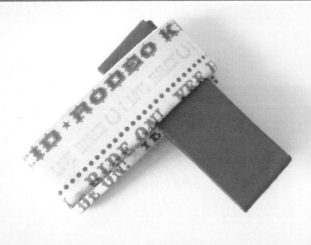

9. Push the inserted piece all the way through, as shown.

10. Insert another piece of folded paper through the last piece added.

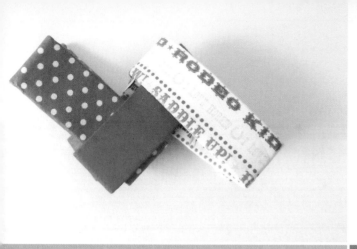

11. Your paper chain should look like this.

12. Continue adding the folded paper, one at a time, until the belt has reached the size needed.

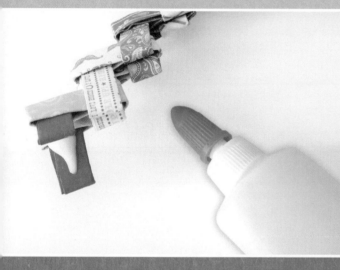

13. Glue together the open ends (at either end of the belt).

14. Attach binder clips over each end, and allow plenty of time to dry.

15. Cut the hook-and-loop fastener into three sections, the same size as the last three pieces of paper on the belt. Glue the loop sides to one end.

16. To finish, stick the hook sides on the last three pieces of paper at the other end of the belt!

67

MATERIALS

empty thread spools x 3,
adhesive paper, wooden skewer, pencil,
black pen, colored pens, white glue,
scissors, tape measure

1.

Measure between the outer rims of
a spool, from top to bottom. Then
measure the circumference,
as shown.

2.

For one spinner, cut out three
pieces of adhesive paper, all the
same height and circumference
as the spool. Sketch three different
characters on each strip, drawing
their heads on one strip, bodies on
the second, and legs and feet on the
third. Color in the characters, then go
over the lines with a black pen.

3.

Remove the backing from the strips
and wrap each one around a spool.

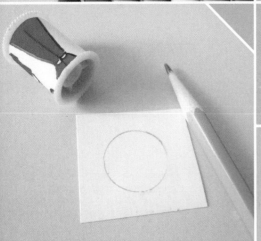

4.

On another piece of adhesive paper,
draw around the base of a spool to
create a circle. Cut out the circle.

5.

Glue the circle at the bottom of
the third spool (the one with the
legs and feet).

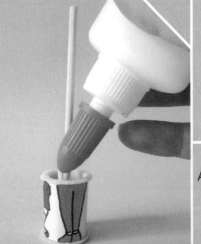

6.

Cut the skewer so that it is ½ in taller
than the three spools stacked on top
of each other. Place the shortened
skewer in the center of the third spool.
Add a good amount of glue to the
hole, making sure that the skewer is
standing up straight. Leave to dry.

7.

Add the other two spools to the skewer,
then turn them to change outfits and
hairstyles. You've made a friend!

STYLISH
SPINNERS

DINO-MITE CHESS GAME

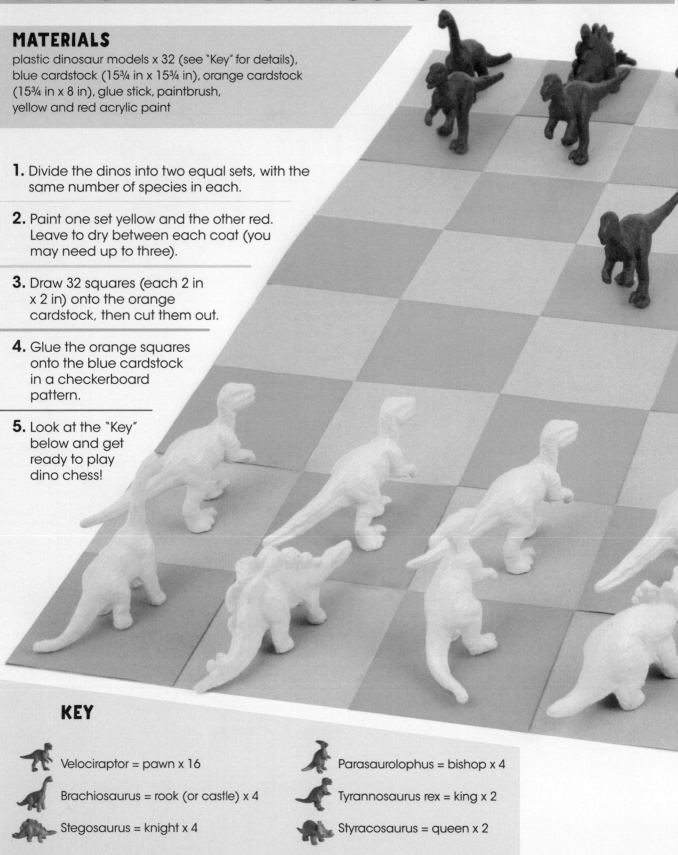

MATERIALS

plastic dinosaur models x 32 (see "Key" for details), blue cardstock (15¾ in x 15¾ in), orange cardstock (15¾ in x 8 in), glue stick, paintbrush, yellow and red acrylic paint

1. Divide the dinos into two equal sets, with the same number of species in each.

2. Paint one set yellow and the other red. Leave to dry between each coat (you may need up to three).

3. Draw 32 squares (each 2 in x 2 in) onto the orange cardstock, then cut them out.

4. Glue the orange squares onto the blue cardstock in a checkerboard pattern.

5. Look at the "Key" below and get ready to play dino chess!

KEY

Velociraptor = pawn x 16

Brachiosaurus = rook (or castle) x 4

Stegosaurus = knight x 4

Parasaurolophus = bishop x 4

Tyrannosaurus rex = king x 2

Styracosaurus = queen x 2

If you're not sure how to play chess, ask an adult to help you look up the rules online.

ROAR!

MATERIALS

grid paper (or if making grid paper: white cardstock, pencil, ruler), brown cardstock, colored embroidery threads, needle, awl, scissors, colored pencils

1.

To make a template, use grid paper or create your own (draw 26 squares across and 24 squares down onto white cardstock—each square to be ¼ in). Then sketch a cupcake onto the grid, coloring the squares as you go.

2.

Fold the brown cardstock in half, then place the cupcake template in the center. Use the awl to push holes through each corner of the colored squares, making sure you only go through the front of the card (and not the back, too).

3.

Continue until all of the holes have been made, revealing a cupcake shape, as shown.

4.

Using your template as a guide, start sewing in the cherry details using a cross-stitch. To do this, bring your needle and thread up and over two diagonal holes, as shown.

5.

Make another diagonal stitch over the top to form a cross, as shown. This is called a cross-stitch!

6.

Continue adding the decorative details (such as the sprinkles) with cross-stitches.

7.

To finish, cross-stitch the main parts of the cake, such as the frosting and cake wrapper. Yum!

72

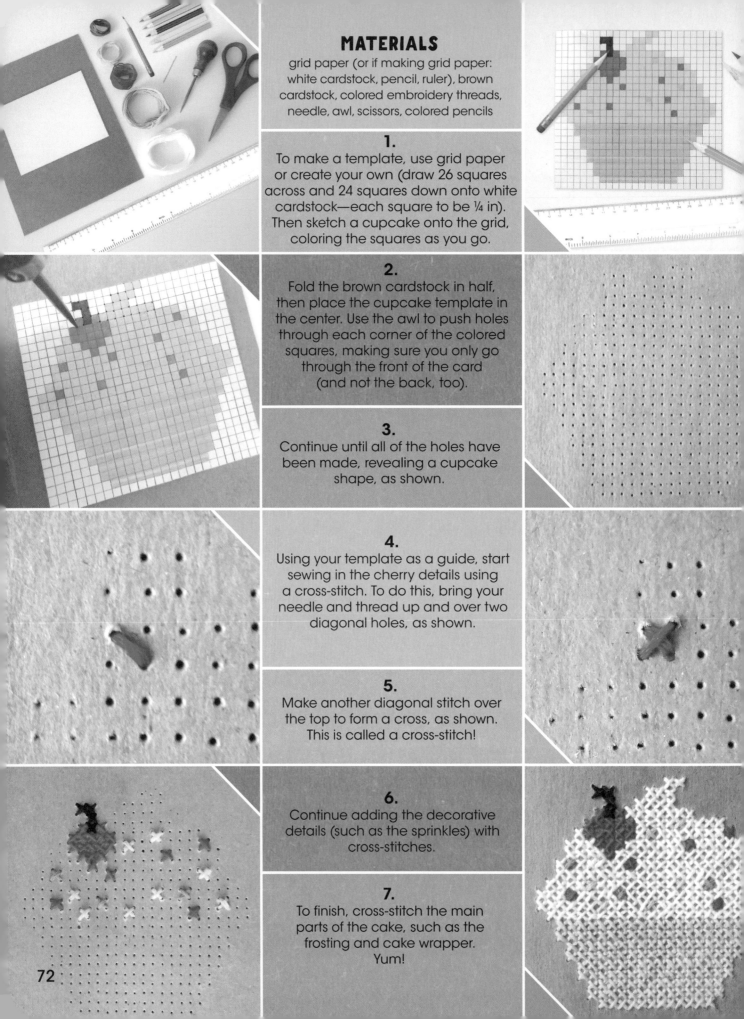

CAKE IT ALL
THE WAY!

SEW-CUTE
CUPCAKE CARD

A lava lamp is a light filled with a colored oily mixture. As the mixture moves up and down, it makes a blobby shape and pattern. Create a similar lava lamp effect with this simple craft!

MATERIALS

water, food coloring, fizzy (dissolving) tablet*, empty glass bottle or jar, vegetable oil

* Ask an adult to help when using the tablet.

1.
Clean the glass bottle (or jar), then fill it ¼ full with water.*

* Ask an adult to clean the bottle (or jar) in a dishwasher or with hot water and dishwashing liquid.

2.
Now pour the oil right up to the neck of the bottle, as shown.

3.
Add a few drops of food coloring, then watch it sink through the oil and mix with the water.

4.
Add a piece of the fizzy tablet to the bottle.* The water will mix with the oil, creating a lava-lamp-like display. Each time the bubbling stops, add another piece of tablet and watch it again!

* Ask an adult to do this!

FIZZY
FUN!

LAVA-LY
BUBBLY
IN A JAR

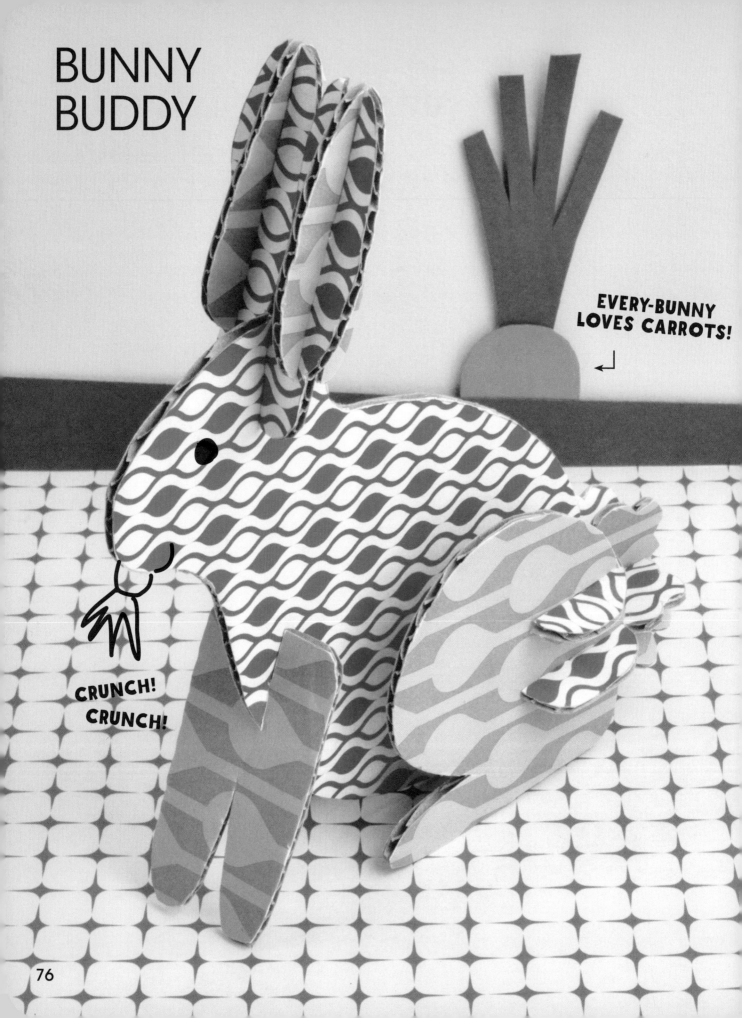

BUNNY BUDDY

EVERY-BUNNY LOVES CARROTS! ↙

CRUNCH! CRUNCH!

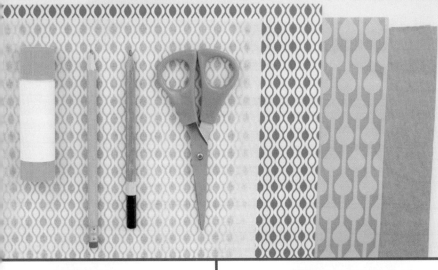

MATERIALS

corrugated cardstock (8½ in x 11 in),
patterned paper x 2 (8½ in x 11 in),
tracing paper (8½ in x 11 in),
number 2 pencil,
soft (number 1) pencil,
glue stick,
scissors,
bunny template (see page 79)

1. Place the tracing paper onto the bunny template, then carefully draw over the outlines with a soft pencil.

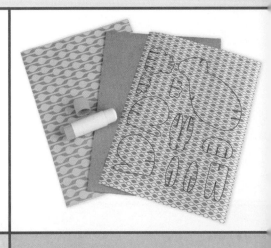

2. Turn the tracing paper over and place it onto a sheet of patterned paper. Now go over the outlines with a number 2 pencil, to transfer them onto the patterned paper.

3. Glue the patterned paper onto the cardstock, then glue another sheet of patterned paper to the other side of the cardstock.

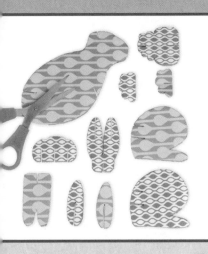

4. Cut out all of the bunny pieces, taking care to follow the pencil lines closely so the pieces will easily slot together.

5. Look at the bunny template as you do the next steps. First find the tail pieces, then fold *Tail 2* and *Tail 3* along the dashed lines to form right angles.

6. Slide *Tail 2* and *Tail 3* (slots b and c) into *Tail 1* (slot a), to make a 3D bunny tail.

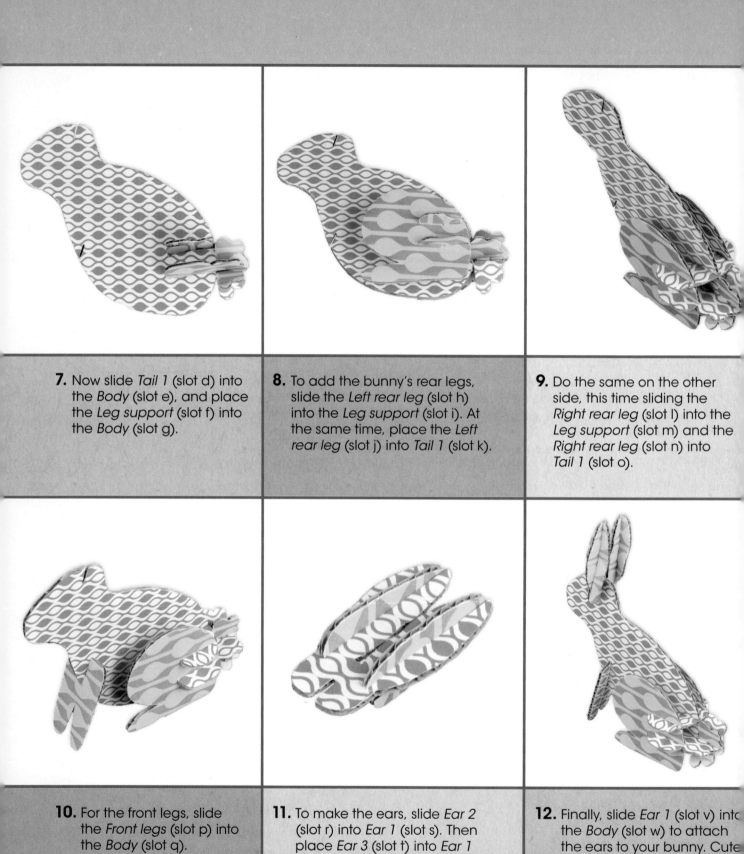

7. Now slide *Tail 1* (slot d) into the *Body* (slot e), and place the *Leg support* (slot f) into the *Body* (slot g).

8. To add the bunny's rear legs, slide the *Left rear leg* (slot h) into the *Leg support* (slot i). At the same time, place the *Left rear leg* (slot j) into *Tail 1* (slot k).

9. Do the same on the other side, this time sliding the *Right rear leg* (slot l) into the *Leg support* (slot m) and the *Right rear leg* (slot n) into *Tail 1* (slot o).

10. For the front legs, slide the *Front legs* (slot p) into the *Body* (slot q).

11. To make the ears, slide *Ear 2* (slot r) into *Ear 1* (slot s). Then place *Ear 3* (slot t) into *Ear 1* (slot u).

12. Finally, slide *Ear 1* (slot v) into the *Body* (slot w) to attach the ears to your bunny. Cute

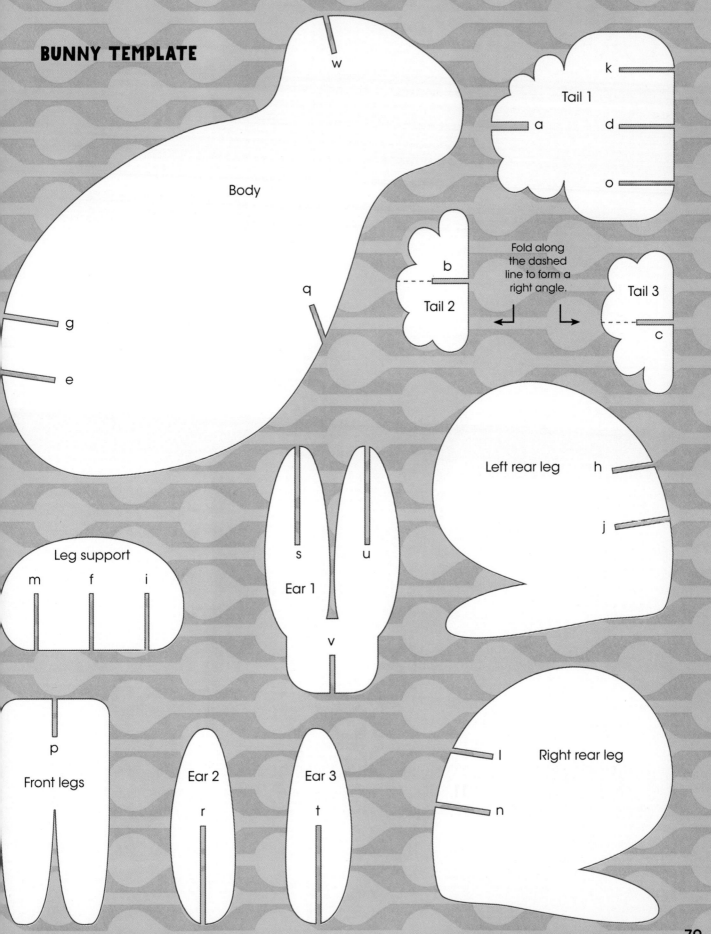

BUNNY TEMPLATE

Body

w

Tail 1

k

a

d

o

q

Fold along
the dashed
line to form a
right angle.

b

Tail 2

Tail 3

c

g

e

Left rear leg

h

j

Leg support

m f i

Ear 1

s u

v

Front legs

p

Ear 2

r

Ear 3

t

Right rear leg

l

n

KATE'S
BEDROOM
↳ KEEP OUT!

MATERIALS
pencil, cardstock, white glue, ruler, scissors, yarn, masking tape

1.
Cut out a strip of cardstock, 4 in x 1 in (or 3 in x ¾ in for smaller pom-poms). Cut a piece of yarn 4 in long and tape it to the cardstock, as shown. Now start wrapping the yarn around the cardstock.

2.
Make sure the cardstock is evenly wrapped and the yarn is not pulled too tight. When you've covered most of the cardstock, tuck the last bit of yarn inside the wrapping and carefully remove the masking tape.

3.
Slide the wrapped yarn off the cardstock, but keep the separate piece of yarn running through the middle. Tie the piece of yarn into a double knot so that the wound yarn bunches into a ball.

4.
Using your scissors, carefully cut through all the loops of yarn until you have a rough circular pom-pom shape.

5.
Trim the edges to neaten up your pom-pom shape. Then repeat the steps until you have lots of different-sized and -colored pom-poms.

6.
Using a ruler and pencil, draw a large letter onto another piece of cardstock, 5 in x 3 in. Then cut it out.

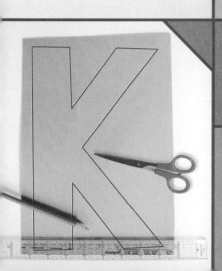

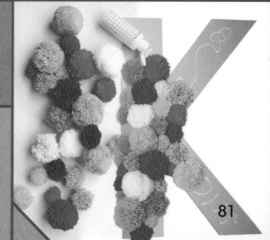

7.
Finally, cover the letter with glue and stick the pom-poms closely together onto the cardstock. Show the world your fluffy letter!

81

FANT-AZTEC LAMPSHADE

The Aztec people were known for creating beautiful art. Brighten up your room with a lampshade inspired by Aztec patterns. For a modern twist, go for super-bright neon colors!

MATERIALS
neon highlighter pens,
black marker,
plain paper lampshade

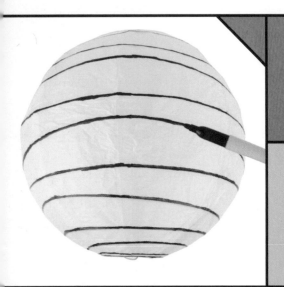

1.
With the marker, draw lines all around the lampshade.

2.
Now add vertical lines up the sides of the lampshade, crossing over the horizontal lines to form sections.

3.
Doodle different patterns in each section. Try spots, stripes, zigzags, or diamonds for Aztec-inspired designs.

4.
Finally, color each pattern with the neon highligher pens. Leave some sections or patterns free from color for an even more dazzling effect.

LIGHT UP
YOUR DOODLES!

MATERIALS

old bath towel,
felt (white, blue, orange),
self-adhesive hook-and-loop fasteners,
ruler,
pencil,
compass,
black marker,
scissors,
needle,
thread,
sewing machine (optional)

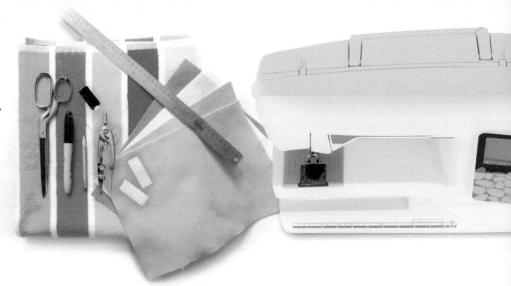

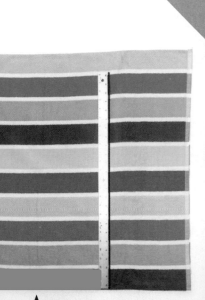

↑ folded edge

1.
Fold the bath towel in half, then use a ruler to measure 24 in from the folded edge. Use the ruler and marker to draw a guide line on the towel.

2.
Now measure 16 in from the left edge of the towel. Carefully cut along the guide lines until you have a smaller rectangle.

16 in

24 in

3.
Draw two curved edges at the fold. then carefully cut off the corners.

4.
To create the monster's eyes, use the compass to draw two 3½-in circles on the blue felt. Then draw two 4½-in circles on the white felt. Cut out the circles.

85

5.
Now sew the blue circles onto the white circles,

6.
Then sew the eyes onto the towel. Make sure only to sew through the top layer of the towel.

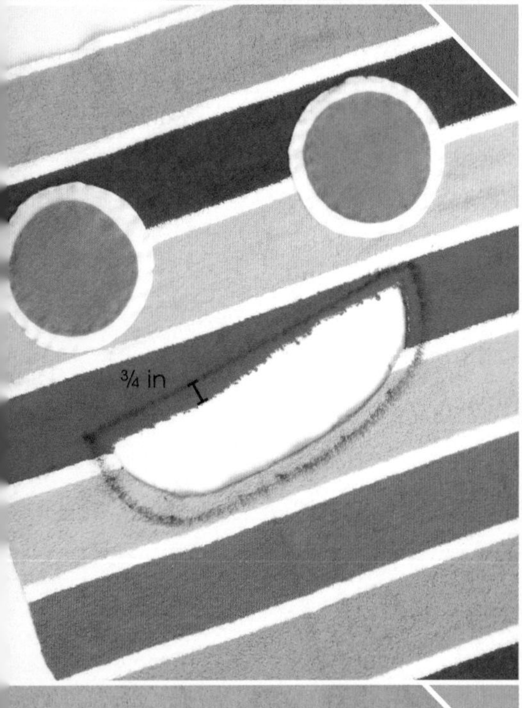

7.
With the marker, draw a large, fun-shaped mouth, making it big enough for your laundry to fit through. Then unfold the towel and cut out the mouth, leaving a ¾-in gap between the pen line and the section to cut out, as shown.

¾ in

8.
Fold the edge back around the mouth, until the pen line is no longer visible, then sew around the mouth, either with the sewing machine or by hand.

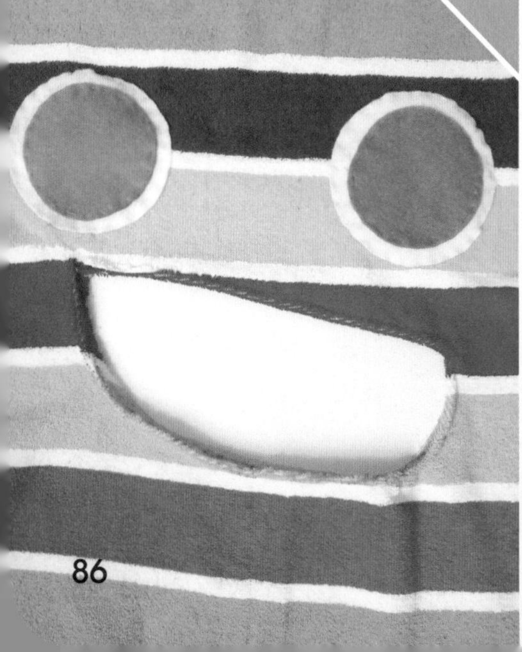

9.
Your monster's mouth should look a bit like the picture on the left.

10.
Place the white felt inside the mouth, then draw on some teeth with a pencil.

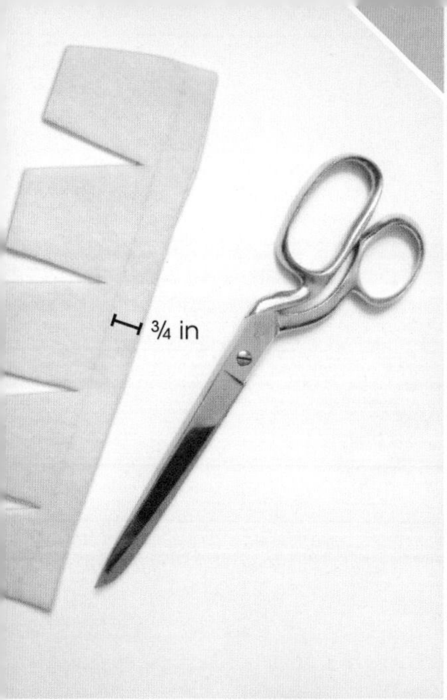

11.
Cut along the pencil marks, leaving a ¾-in gap at the top.

12.
Sew the teeth inside the mouth, either with the sewing machine or by hand. Now turn the towel inside out, with the seams showing.

13.
Stitch around the three (unfolded) sides of the towel. Then pull the towel back through the monster's mouth so the seams are on the inside again.

14.
Cut out a pair of feet and arms from the yellow felt.

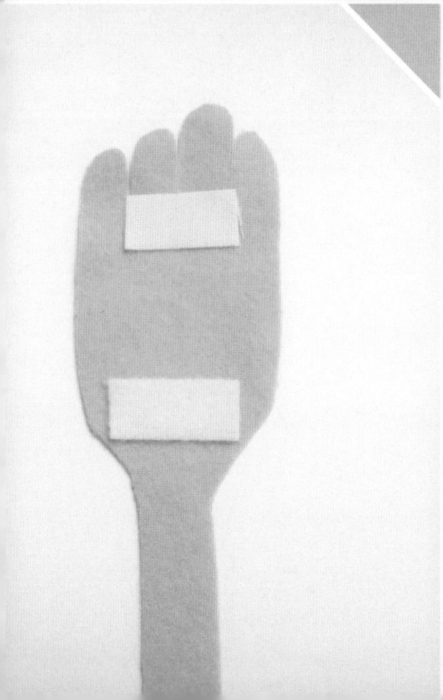

15.
Cut out two pieces from the hook-and-loop fastener. Separate the hook from the loop, then stitch them on opposite sides of the monster's hand. Repeat on the other hand.

16.
Sew the arms and feet to the back of the towel. Now place the hands over a rail or towel rack and fold the fingers down until the hook-and-loop fasteners stick together. Grrrrreat!

¾ in

Keep your secrets under wraps in this pretty patterned diary. Just grab some ribbon and glue, and get weaving!

MATERIALS
plain diary (or notebook), blue ribbon, silver ribbon, all-purpose glue, scissors

1.
Measure the width of the front cover. Cut the silver ribbon into strips, each 1 in longer than this measurement. Now measure the length of the front cover. Cut the blue ribbon into strips, each 1 in longer than this measurement.

2.
Lay the ribbon strips side by side on the front cover to check that you have enough. Now glue one side of each silver strip (½ in in from the edge) down the length of the inside cover.

3.
Repeat until all the silver ribbon has been glued to the top of the inside cover, then leave to dry. Now add some glue to the spine. Pull each strip of silver ribbon across the front of the book, gluing in place on the spine. Once the glue has dried, trim any excess length of ribbon.

4.
Now glue one side of each blue strip (½ in in from the edge) along the width of the inside cover, as shown. Then leave to dry.

5.
Weave the blue ribbon in and out of the silver ribbon, making any pattern you choose.

6.
Once you have completed your pattern, glue the blue ribbon to the bottom of the inside cover to finish. Why not create a smaller ribbon weave notebook to match?

SHH!
TOP SECRET!

MATERIALS
pair of socks, scissors, needle, thread, buttons x 2, felt, black marker

phone inside

1.
Turn one sock inside out, then slide your phone inside, just above the ankle. Mark a line ½ in below where your phone sits.

2.
Remove the phone, then sew the two layers of the sock together, following the mark made in step 1.

3.
Now trim off the sock foot, ½ in below the stitched line.

4.
Use the stitched sock as a guide for the other sock, but make it 1 in shorter. Turn the socks around the right way, so the stitching is on the inside.

5.
Sew a button on each side of the elastic area of the small, outer sock. Push the larger sock inside the smaller one.

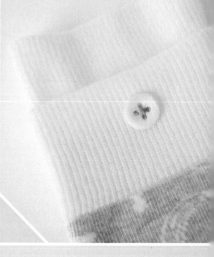

6.
Cut a strip of felt long enough to stretch from one button to the other, going over the top of both socks. Measure carefully and snip a slot at each end of the felt, to make buttonholes.

7.
Slide both buttons through the buttonholes, making sure the felt wraps over the top of your cozy phone case.

ROCK YOUR
SOCKS OFF!

TOTALLY EMOJI BALLS

Keep fidgeting fingers busy with these cute sensory balls. Give each character a different expression to match how you feel!

MATERIALS
flour,
plastic food bag,
scissors,
spoon,
white balloon,
red balloon,
black marker

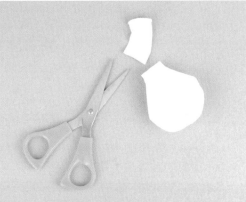

1. Partially fill the plastic food bag with flour, making sure it's not too big to hold in your hand. Tie a double knot at the top, letting out air as you go. Cut the bag above the knot.

2. Then snip the narrow end or "neck" off the white balloon. Leave ¼ in of the "neck" on the wider section, as shown.

3. Push the bag of flour inside the white balloon, knotted end first. Squash the balloon into a round ball.

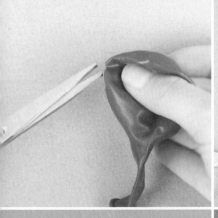

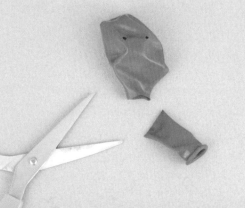

4. Flatten the red balloon, then snip it twice to create a hole near the wider end of the balloon. This will be an eye.

5. Repeat step 4 to snip another hole for the other eye. When flattened, the holes in the balloon should look quite small. Repeat step 2, then stretch the red balloon over the white ball.

6. The eye holes should now be bigger. Draw pupils, then add eyebrows and a mouth. Repeat steps 1 to 5 to create more emoji characters. Make the eye holes bigger or smaller for different expressions.

MATERIALS

craft sticks, embroidery threads, glass (or jar), white glue, pan of boiling water

1. Place the craft sticks in a pan of boiling water for 30 minutes. Carefully remove the sticks from the pan, then leave to cool (but not dry out) before the next step.*

* Ask an adult to do all of this for you.

2. The sticks should now be soft enough to bend into curves. Do this slowly, so the sticks don't snap.

3. Place each curved stick into the base of a small cup and leave overnight to dry. This will help form a cuff shape.

4. Add some glue to the inside of each curved stick (arm cuff). Tightly wrap some thread around the cuff, as shown. Start a little way in from one end of each cuff.

5. To change thread colors, snip off the previous thread, then add the new color next to it, as shown. Finish a little way in from the end, then snip away any excess thread. Add more glue if necessary.

STICK-ERRIFIC ARM CUFFS

DROP THREAD GORGEOUS!

PICTURE HOLDERS

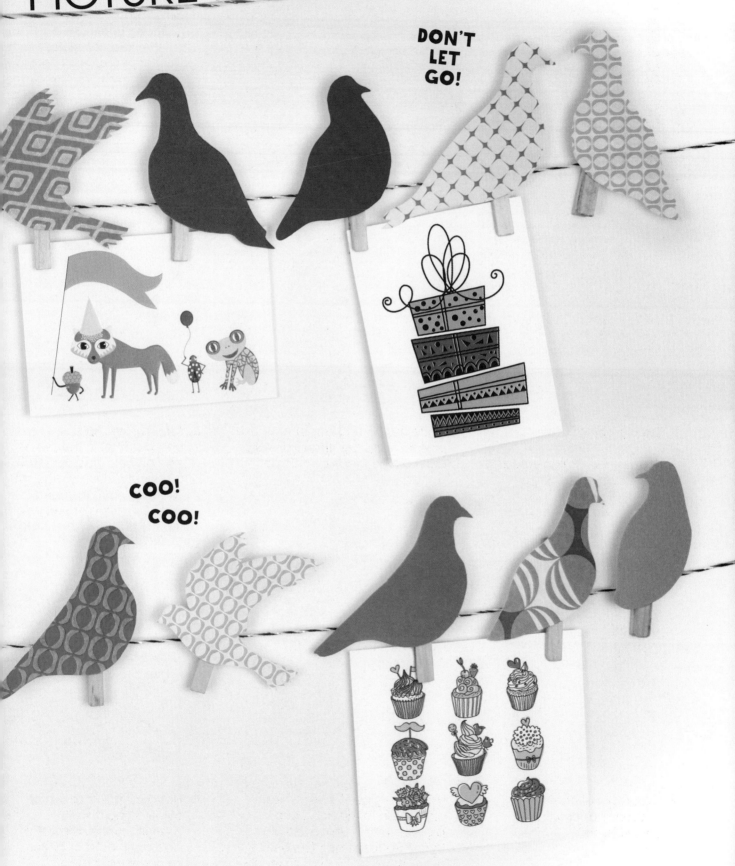

DON'T
LET
GO!

COO!
COO!

MATERIALS
colored paper,
patterned paper,
white cardstock (8½ in x 11 in),
tracing paper (8½ in x 11 in),
pigeon templates (right),
scissors,
wooden clothespins,
soft (number 1) pencil,
number 2 pencil,
glue stick,
white glue,
string

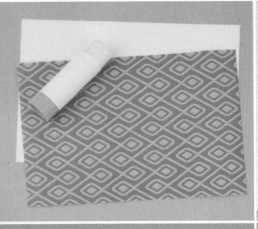

1. Cut a piece of white cardstock in half, then glue a sheet of patterned paper to the back.

2. Place the tracing paper on the pigeon template, then carefully draw over the outlines with a soft pencil.

3. Turn the tracing paper over and place it on the plain side of the cardstock. Now go over two of the pigeon outlines with a number 2 pencil, to transfer them onto the cardstock.

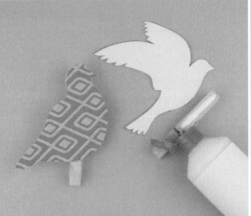

4. Carefully cut out the pigeon shapes with your scissors.

5. Use white glue to attach each clothespin to the back of a pigeon shape. Leave the glue to dry. Repeat steps 1 to 5 to make more clothespin pigeons.

6. Hang up a line or two of twine along a wall.* Clip the pigeons to the twine, then add a gift card or picture beneath each one.

* Ask an adult for help!

PIGEON TEMPLATES

ZIP-MOUTH MONSTERS

ZIP
IT!

silicone cake molds x 2
(each the same size),
zipper (same length as
circumference of
cake molds),
craft foam,
black pen,
all-purpose glue,*
needle,
thread,
scissors

↙

* Ask for an adult's help with the all-purpose glue in step 4!

1. Using a running stitch, sew one side of the zipper along the inside rim of a cake mold. Try to sew as close to the zipper as possible.

2. Unzip the zipper, then sew the unstitched side around the rim of the second cake mold. Place it on top of the other mold.

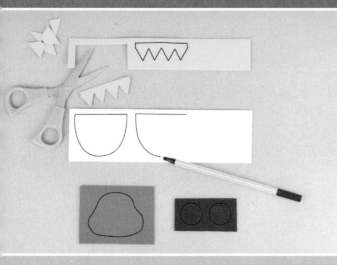

3. Draw eyes, eyebrows, and a nose on your craft foam, then cut them out.

4. Glue the features onto the base of the upside down cake mold. Now create some more monster friends for your zip-mouth monster.

WASHI TAPE MAKEOVERS

From single strips to diagonal stripes, let washi tape work its magic and give everyday items a new lease on life!

Jazz up boring binder clips with brightly colored washi tape! Just cut them to size and stick them on. Simple!

Transform a cup into a pencil holder with a dazzling diagonal design.

Decorate clothespins washi-tape style, then use them as note holders and picture hangers, or add magnets to the back and stick them on your fridge!

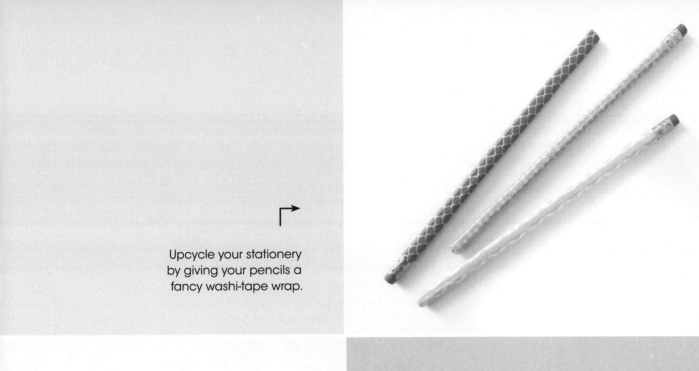

Upcycle your stationery by giving your pencils a fancy washi-tape wrap.

There's no need to spend money on new photo frames ... Revamp yours with alternating strips of tape, like this!

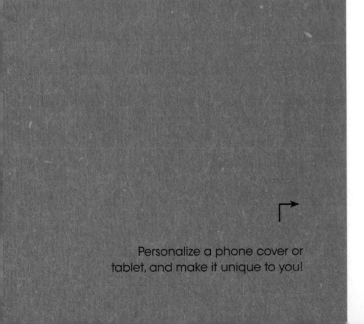

Personalize a phone cover or tablet, and make it unique to you!

103

MATERIALS
yellow felt, cream felt, zipper
(same length as width of felt),
pencil, scissors, needle, pin, thread

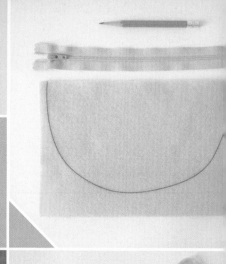

1.
Fold the yellow felt in half and draw a semicircle next to the open edge (opposite the folded edge), the same width as the zipper. Cut out both layers of felt, so you end up with two semicircles.

2.
Now draw around one of the semicircles onto the cream felt. Draw another semicircle inside it, making it ½ in smaller all around, then cut out the smaller semicircle. Next, cut out four triangles from more yellow felt. These need to be small enough to fit inside the cream felt.

3.
Sew the yellow triangles onto the cream felt with a running stitch.

4.
Now sew the cream felt onto one of the yellow semicircles. The felt should start to look like a fruit segment.

5.
Sew both yellow semicircles on either side of the zipper, leaving ¼ in between the top edge of each piece of felt and the teeth of the zipper, as shown.

6.
Fold the fruit in half so that the edges of the two semicircles line up. Tuck in the excess zipper on each side, and pin in place.

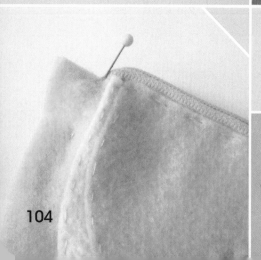

7.
Starting at the top left corner, next to the zipper, stitch the felt all the way around and back to the zipper on the other side, making sure to sew in the zipper ends. Remove all pins, then make more fruity pouches!

CUTIE FRUITY FELT POUCHES

MADE WITH
ZEST!

TISSUE BOX CLOCK

AH-AH-AH-TWEET-CHOO!

TICK TOCK!

MATERIALS

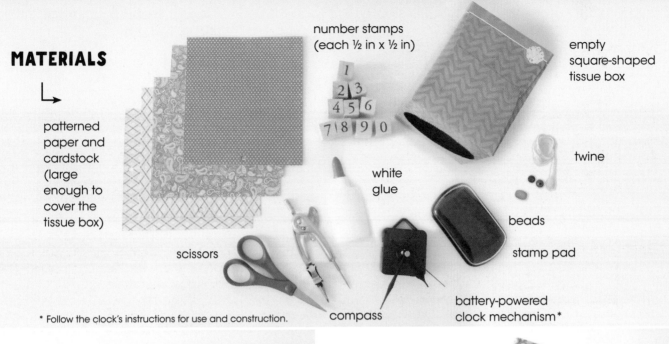

patterned paper and cardstock (large enough to cover the tissue box)

number stamps (each ½ in x ½ in)

empty square-shaped tissue box

twine

white glue

beads

stamp pad

scissors

compass

battery-powered clock mechanism*

* Follow the clock's instructions for use and construction.

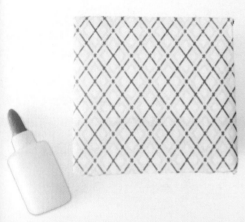

1. Glue a sheet of patterned paper to the bottom of the tissue box.

2. Cover all four sides of the box with a different sheet of patterned paper. Leave the top of the box (the side with the opening) uncovered.

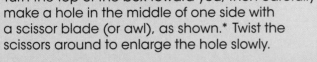

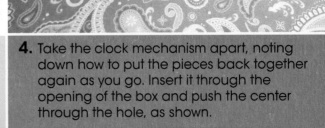

3. Turn the top of the box toward you, then carefully make a hole in the middle of one side with a scissor blade (or awl), as shown.* Twist the scissors around to enlarge the hole slowly.

* Ask an adult to do this for you.

4. Take the clock mechanism apart, noting down how to put the pieces back together again as you go. Insert it through the opening of the box and push the center through the hole, as shown.

107

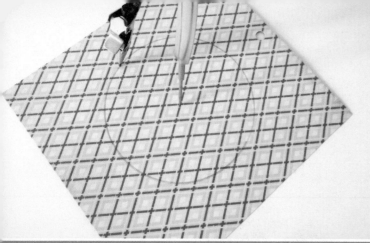

5. On another sheet of patterned paper, draw a circle with your compass slightly smaller than the width of the box. Cut out the circle, then use the blade to make a hole in the middle.

6. Glue the circle over the box, gently pushing the clock mechanism through the hole in the circular sheet of patterned paper.

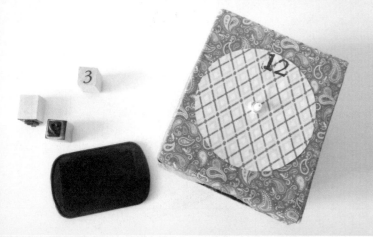

7. Turn the box so the opening is now at the bottom, then stamp numbers around the inside of the circle. Start with 12 at the top, then 6 at the bottom, and add 3 and 9 on either side. Fill in the gaps with the other numbers.

8. Add and tighten the remaining clock parts on the mechanism, so that your clock starts to take shape.

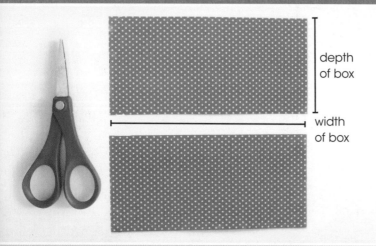

depth of box

width of box

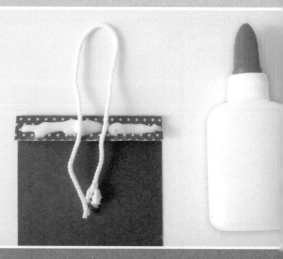

9. For the roof, cut a piece of patterned cardstock into two pieces. These should be the same width as the front face of the box and slightly narrower than the depth of the box.

10. Create a tab on one roof piece by folding back the top edge by ½ in. Cut a 6-in piece of twine and form a loop as shown. Place the loop in the center of the tab and add glue across the top.

11. Place the other strip over the top, press down firmly, then leave to dry. Trim the bottom edge of this strip to line up with the one underneath.

12. Cut another 6-in piece of twine and thread three beads along the length. Tie a double knot below each bead to keep them in place. Feed the unknotted end of twine into the bottom of the box and glue it to the inside wall.

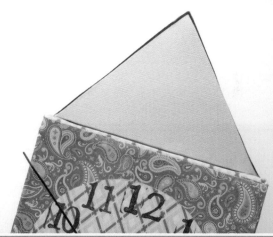

13. To attach the roof to the box, glue the edges on either side of the box (½ in in from each edge).

14. To finish the roof, draw a triangle the same size and shape as the roof sides on a piece of cardstock. Add a tab to each side of the triangle and cut out. Fold the tabs back and glue them inside the roof section.

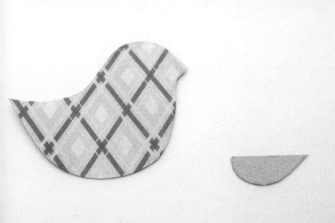

15. Draw a bird shape and wing on different-patterned and -colored cardstock. Make the bird ⅓ the size of the width of the tissue box. Cut out the pieces.

16. Glue the bird wing to the body and then glue the body to the roof of the clock house. Now hang up your clock!

SEWING PIN DREAMCATCHER

IT'S SEW DREAMY!

MATERIALS

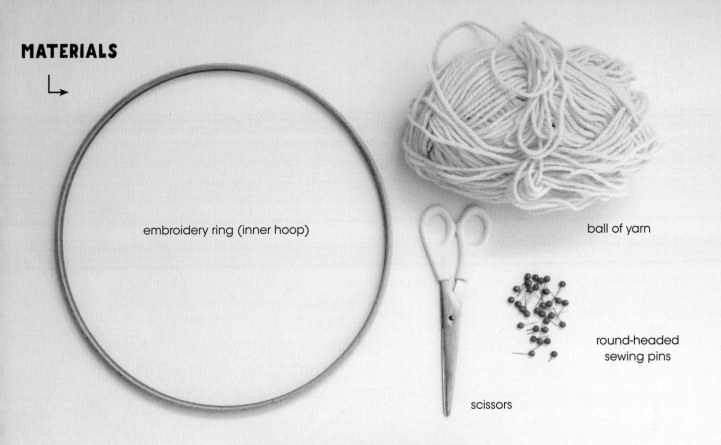

embroidery ring (inner hoop)

ball of yarn

round-headed
sewing pins

scissors

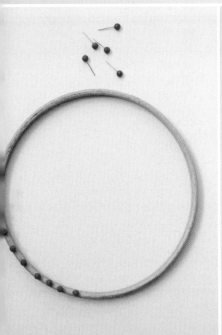

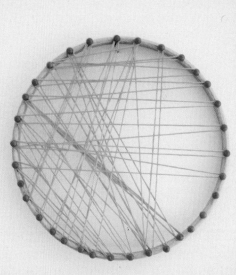

1. Push the pins firmly into the hoop, ½ in apart.*

* Ask an adult to help you.

2. Wind the yarn around the first pin, then loop the yarn around a pin on the other side of the ring, tying a double knot to secure.

3. Keep weaving the yarn back and forth, looping it around each pin (some more than once) until you are happy with the pattern. Tie a double knot around the last pin, to secure the yarn in place. Cut off the ends with your scissors. Sweet dreams!

SEAFARIN' PET PHOTO BOOTH

MATERIALS

poster paints,
black marker,
paintbrush,
large cardboard box (slightly
bigger than your pet),
scissors,
dinner plate,
pencil,
all-purpose glue

1. Cut off the back of the cardboard box and put it aside for later. Unfold the top and bottom of the box, then flatten the remaining sides.

2. Place a large plate at the front of the box, 2 in down from the top. This will act as a rough template for the size of hole you need for your pet's head to poke through. Draw around the plate.*

3. Now sketch the face of a bearded pirate, or sea captain, around the plate template. The face doesn't have to be the exact same shape as the template, but it should be no smaller. Leave out the facial features.

4. Draw the character's body, arms, legs, and feet, then add paint and leave to dry.

5. Using the marker, go over the outlines to make your pirate or captain stand out.

6. Now carefully cut out your character's face, leaving the beard intact.

7. Draw a funny hat on the spare piece of cardboard, then paint it. Go over the outlines with the marker when dry. Cut it out, then glue the hat above the head on the box.

8. Stand up your seafarin' photo booth and guide your pet inside. Happy snapping!

* The hole in the box needs to be large enough for your pet's head, to be sure it won't get stuck! Enlarge if necessary.

MATERIALS
cardstock circles x 2 (3½ in in diameter with 1 in hole in the center), green felt, green yarn, red yarn, scissors, white glue

1.
Cut a piece of red yarn 195 in long. Place the two rings together and wind the red yarn through the center hole until the yarn no longer fits through.

2.
Insert the scissors between the cardstock rings and trim the yarn all the way around.

3.
Slip another piece of yarn between the rings, and pull the ends tightly together. Tie it in a double knot.

4.
Now remove the cardstock discs, and scrunch the yarn to form a pom-pom.

5.
Trim the pom-pom into a cherry shape. Repeat steps 1 to 4 to make another two cherries.

6.
Cut out three pieces of dark green yarn (each 6 in long).

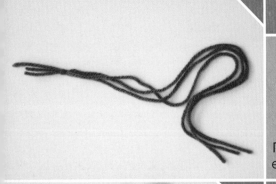

7.
Braid the yarn by tying the strands together at one end, then cross the strand on the left over the one in the middle. Now cross the strand on the right over the one in the middle. Repeat the process until you reach the end of the yarn, then tie a double knot.

8.
Make another two cherry stems, following step 7. Then cut out some leaf shapes from green felt.

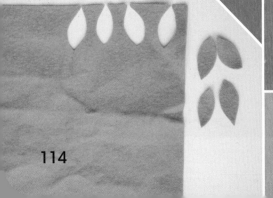

9.
Glue the pom-poms and leaves onto the stems, as shown, then leave to dry. Finally, tie the cherries onto the handle of a bag!

114

SO CHERRY CUTE! →

POM-POM CHERRY CHARMS

A-MAZE-ING MARBLE GAME

AVOID
THE
TRAPS!

MATERIALS
shoebox cover,
dark blue paper (large enough
to fit inside the shoebox cover),
construction paper
(light blue, yellow, white,
red, and black),
colored craft sticks,
pencil,
compass,
scissors,
ruler,
glue stick,
glue gun,
marble

↵

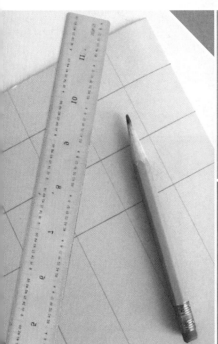

1.
Draw 48 squares (each 1 in
x 1 in) onto the pale blue
construction paper, then
cut them out.

2.
Glue the pale blue squares
onto the dark blue paper in a
checkerboard pattern.

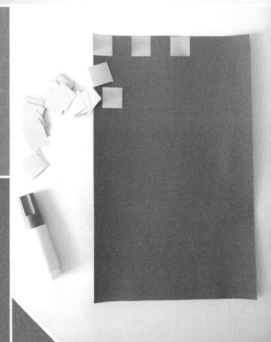

3.
Repeat until you have covered
the entire sheet.

4.
Now use your compass to draw the
following circles on the other sheets of
construction paper:
five red and two black
(each 1¾ in in diameter),
five white and two yellow
(each 1½ in in diameter),
five red (each 1¼ in in diameter)
and one black (½ in in diameter).

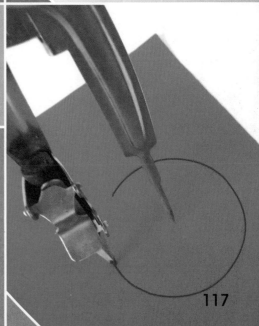

117

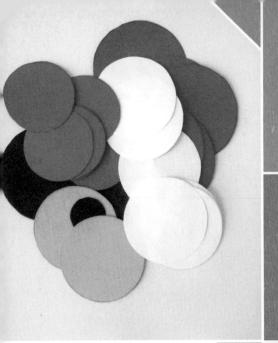

5.
Next, carefully cut out all of the circles from the construction paper.

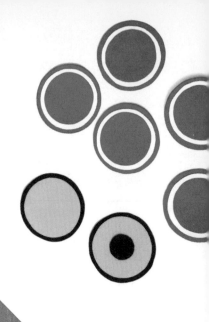

6.
Glue the different circles together, matching the colors and sizes to the picture on the right. You should end up with seven circles in total.

7.
Use the compass to draw another circle in the middle of each red-and-white circle (¾ in in diameter). Then cut them out. These will be the traps!

8.
Place the checkerboard inside the shoebox cover (but don't glue it down just yet, as you'll need to cut out holes for the "traps" in step 11). Glue the yellow-and-black circles on top, as shown. These are the start and finish points of your maze game.

9.
Now place the red-and-white circles in the same positions as pictured on the left, but don't glue them down.

10.
Use a pencil to trace around the inside of each hole onto the checkerboard, as shown. Then remove the red-and-white circles.

11.
Remove the checkerboard from the shoebox cover, then cut out inside the circles you have just drawn, to make holes. Now glue the checkerboard to the shoebox cover.

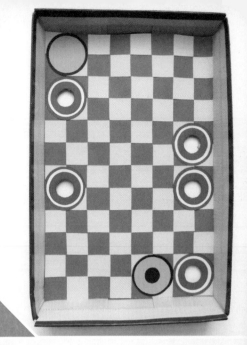

12.
Glue the red-and-white circles over the holes in the checkerboard, but make sure the holes are still visible.

13.
To create the walls of the maze, use the glue gun to run glue along one side of a craft stick.*

* Ask an adult to use the glue gun in this step.

14.
Place the craft stick into position, as shown. Hold it in place for a few minutes until the glue is dry.

15.
Use the scissors to make shorter craft sticks, as shown, then repeat steps 13 to 14.

16.
Continue adding walls until your maze is complete. Write START on the yellow-and-black circle at the top, and FINISH on the one at the bottom. Place a marble on START, then tilt the game around as you guide your marble to the FINISH!

MATERIALS
black and blond bobby pins x 240, jewelry wire, jewelry clasp and ring, jewelry pliers, wire clippers

1.
Cut three pieces of wire to the following lengths: 21 in, 25 in, and 33 in. Slip eight black bobby pins over the middle of the shortest piece of wire. Now add three blond bobby pins to each side, as shown.

2.
Repeat step 1 until you have nine black bobby pin sections and ten blond bobby pin sections on the same piece of wire.

3.
Do the same on the two remaining pieces of wire, but alternate the patterns however you like.

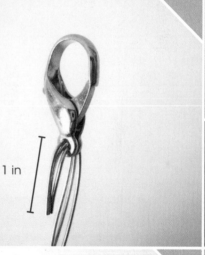

1 in

4.
Now line up all three wires, then insert the ends on the left through the jewelry clasp. Fold the wires over, 1 in down from the clasp.

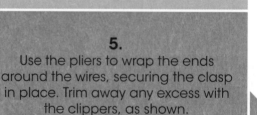

5.
Use the pliers to wrap the ends around the wires, securing the clasp in place. Trim away any excess with the clippers, as shown.

6.
Now insert the other end of the wires through the ring. Fold them over 1 in down from the ring, then use the pliers to wrap the ends around the wires, securing the ring in place. Trim off any excess.

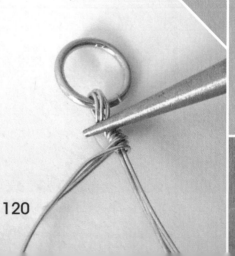

7.
Finally, secure the bobby pins in place by wrapping a small piece of wire around each side of the first line, as shown.

BOBBY PIN
NECKLACE

↑
*GET HOOKED
ON NECKWEAR!*

121

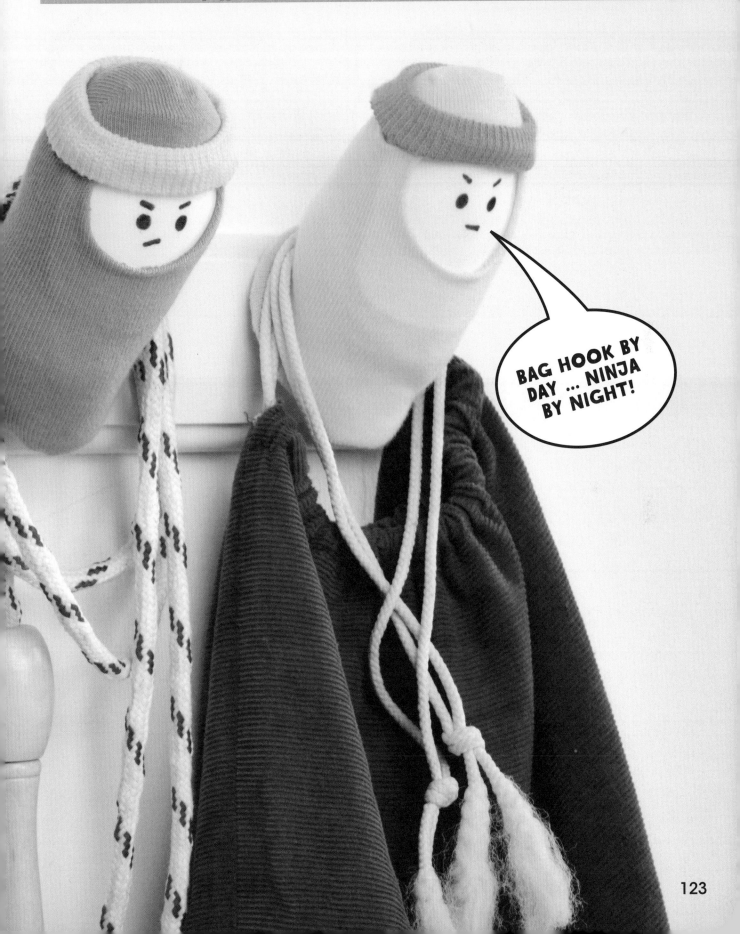

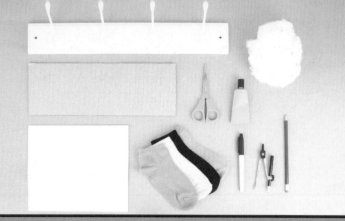

MATERIALS

coat hook rail, cardstock, white craft foam,
ankle socks x 4, scissors, toy stuffing, all-purpose glue*,
black marker, compass, pencil

* Ask an adult to help use the all-purpose glue in steps 3 and 9!

1. Cut the ankle seam (or ribbed edging) off each sock and put them aside for later.

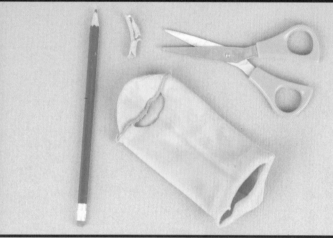

2. Turn one sock inside out and draw a semicircle just below the toe seam. Cut it out.

3. Run a trail of all-purpose glue around the edge of the semicircle. Fold the rough edges back and press into the glue.

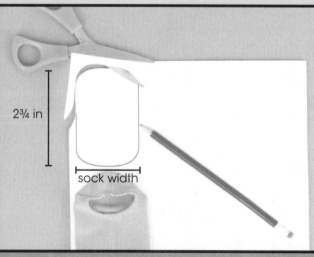

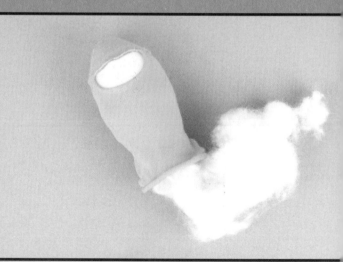

2¾ in

sock width

4. Draw a rounded rectangle onto the white craft foam, 2¾ in long and the same width as the sock. Cut it out.

5. Turn the sock the right side out and place the white craft foam in front of the semicircle. Fill the sock with stuffing behind the craft foam, and leave a gap at the end.

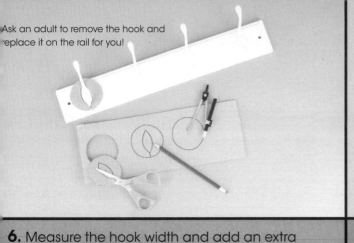

6. Measure the hook width and add an extra ½ in. Using the compass, draw and cut out a cardstock circle matching this size. Remove the hook from the rail, then trace around the base in the center of the circle.* Snip a slot at the bottom of the circle, then cut out the shape.

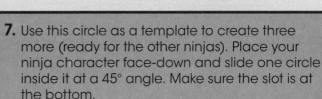

7. Use this circle as a template to create three more (ready for the other ninjas). Place your ninja character face-down and slide one circle inside it at a 45° angle. Make sure the slot is at the bottom.

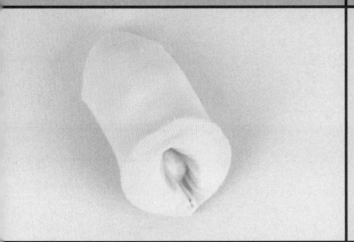

8. Tuck the end of the sock inside the hole. Use your fingers to push the sock and stuffing down, to keep the hole open.

9. Now choose a sock seam from step 1 to create the headband. Roll the sock seam so that any rough edges are hidden inside, then glue it to the ninja's head, above its face.

10. Draw a ninja face on the white craft foam with your marker.

11. Repeat steps 2 to 5 for the other three socks. Then slot the cardstock shapes made in step 7 inside the ninjas, and repeat steps 8 to 10. Slide your ninjas over the hooks, then hang up the rail, ready to use.*

* Ask an adult to do this for you!

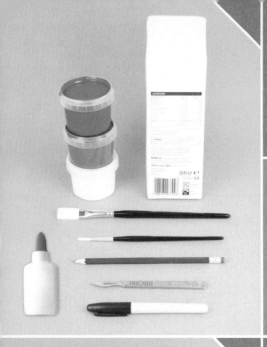

MATERIALS

empty juice carton, acrylic paints (white, blue, and orange), paintbrushes, pencil, craft knife, black marker, white glue

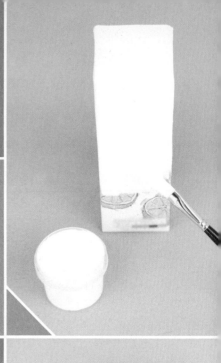

1.

Make sure the juice carton is empty, then glue the spout down.* Add two coats of white acrylic paint, allowing to dry between each coat.

* Ask an adult to rinse the carton thoroughly with water and dishwashing liquid.

2.

Use a pencil to sketch the design of your shop onto the sides of the carton.

3.

Paint over the pencil in blue and orange. Don't worry about being too neat at this stage.

4.

Now use your marker to carefully draw around the outlines and fill in the details.

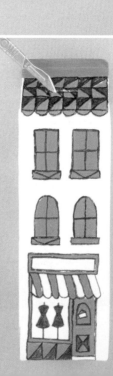

5.

Use the craft knife to cut a small slot in the top of the carton to pop your money through.* Happy saving!

* Ask an adult to do this for you.

STASH YOUR CASH!

SAVING SHOP

COOL
CARTON
MONEY
BOX

STRING-MÂCHÉ GARLAND

↑ IT'S A STRING THING!

MATERIALS

colored string, balloons x 8, white glue, water, bowl, large deep bowl, long wooden skewer, scissors, ruler (12 in long)

1.

Cut out a length of string, 200 in in total. Tie a slip knot at one end. Mix ¾ white glue with ¼ water in a bowl. Now place the string in the mixture, leaving the slip knot end out of the bowl.

2.

Inflate one of the balloons to 5 in long and tie a knot at the end. Next loop the string's slip knot over the knot of the balloon.

3.

Carefully wrap the glue-covered string around the balloon. Feed the string through your fingers, to remove any excess glue as you go.

4.

Keep wrapping until all of the string is used. Tuck the end of the string under another piece of string, to secure it in place.

5.

Next thread the skewer carefully through the knot at the top of the balloon. Be careful not to puncture the balloon! Then hang it over a large bowl. Wait until the glue is clear and dry (this will take a few hours).

6.

Use the skewer to pop the balloon, then remove the balloon from the string ball. Repeat steps 1 to 6 until you have eight string balls.

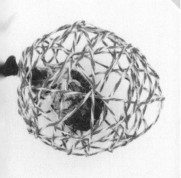

7.

Cut a 80-in piece of string and thread through the slip knot loop of one ball. Now slide the ball along the piece of string, leaving 12 in at the end. Tie double knots on either side, to keep the ball in place. Continue to add more balls, placing them 8 in apart from each other, until you have finished the garland.

TAPE-OMIZED CABLES 'N' CASES

Give your gadgets a tape-over with these simple ideas, using versatile duct tape!*

RING!
RING!

STRIPE-SATIONAL!

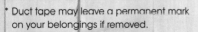

* Duct tape may leave a permanent mark on your belongings if removed.

Jazz up an old pair of earphones by winding a long, thin piece of duct tape around the cable, creating a fab 'n' funky spiral pattern.

Bring your charger up to date with a cool color-block pattern. Just cut two contrasting colored tapes into chunky square pieces, then wrap them around the cord, alternating the colors as you go!

For a dazzling, stripy tablet case, try alternating colored tape with thick and thin strips, and opt for a diagonal pattern. To make your tablet really zing, leave a small gap between each strip! Don't forget to trim off the edges to finish.

Upcycle your phone case with a super-stylish chevron pattern! Place a rectangular piece of tape at the base of the phone, then overlap different-colored triangular pieces all the way to the top. You've got it covered!

IN-THE-FRAME LAMPSHADE

LET IT GLOW!

MATERIALS
frames with plastic panes x 4, white glue, food coloring, small empty plastic bottles, scissors, all-purpose glue, lamp base, black cardstock, paper

1.
Clean the bottles, then squeeze some glue into each one. Next add 8 tsp of food coloring—one color per bottle. Screw the caps on tightly and shake each bottle thoroughly to mix.

2.
Remove the plastic panes from the frames. Cover your work area with a plastic sheet or newspaper and then squeeze the colored glue from each bottle onto the plastic panes.

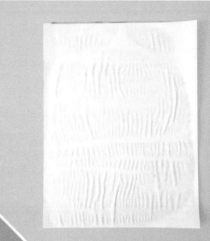

3.
Place a sheet of paper on top and gently spread the colored glue around. Remove the paper and leave the pane to dry. Repeat steps 2 and 3 for the other panes.

4.
On the back of a frame, dot some glue in each corner. Place a pane onto the glue and press down firmly so the pane sticks to the frame. Repeat for the other frames and panes.

5.
Cut the black cardstock into four long strips, all the same length as the longer sides of the frame and around 1 in wide.

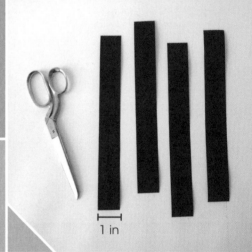

1 in

of black cardstock

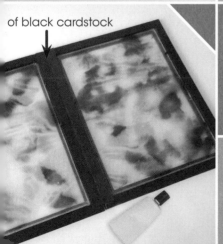

6.
Place two frames side by side, then glue a strip of black cardstock over the two touching edges to join. Repeat for the other two frames, then join the two coupled frames together (side by side) with a third strip of black cardstock.

7.
Stand the frames up in a cube, with the cardstock strips on the inside. Glue the final strip to the two unjoined edges. Now place over your lamp!

final strip of black cardstock

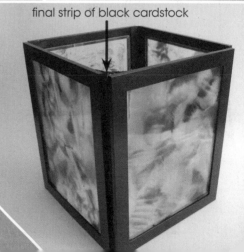

MATERIALS

sticky back plastic, photo,
glitter stars and flakes, scissors,
clean jar with lid,* water

*Ask an adult to clean the jar in a dishwasher
or with hot water and dishwashing liquid.

1.
Cover both sides of the photo with
sticky back plastic, as shown.

2.
Trim the edges, but make
sure the photo is completely
covered with plastic.

MAKE THEM
SPARKLE!

GLITTER STORM PHOTOS

3.
Place the photo upside down inside the jar and at the back. Add the glitter stars and flakes.

4.
Fill the jar with water, and put the lid on tightly.

5.
Shake your jar and enjoy your fab photo glitter storm!

ELE-BOX
BOOKENDS

ELEPHANT-ASTIC!

Keep your books from falling off the shelf with these fab 'n' functional elephant bookends!

MATERIALS
newspaper, masking tape, sealed plastic food bags filled with uncooked rice, colored paper, water, bowl, white glue, all-purpose glue,* pencil, paintbrush, scissors, wrapping paper, cereal boxes

* Ask an adult to help use the all-purpose glue in steps 9, 10, and 14!

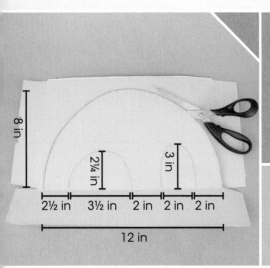

8 in

2¼ in

3 in

2½ in 3½ in 2 in 2 in 2 in

12 in

1.
For one side of the elephant's body, draw a semicircle onto an opened-out cereal box. Sketch two smaller semicircles inside it for the legs and trunk (see measurements on the left). Then cut along the pencil lines.

2.
Use this as a template to trace the other side of the elephant onto another box. Then cut it out.

2 in

3.
Next cut out three squares from the cereal box cardstock. Each square will need to be 2 in in height and the same width as the legs and trunk. Tape in place on one side, at the bottom, as shown. Repeat for the other side of the elephant.

4.
Cut a strip of cardstock 2 in wide, making sure it's long enough to curve over the top of the elephant's body. Secure in place with lots of small pieces of tape, as shown.

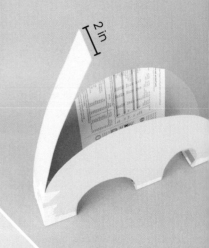

2 in

2 in

2 in

5.
Cut a shorter strip of cardstock, again 2 in wide, and tape it to the inside of the legs, as shown.

6.
Take the plastic food bags (containing uncooked rice), and place them inside the elephant to give it weight. Continue to add bags of rice until the inside of the elephant is full. Now tape a strip of cardstock (2 in wide) between the front legs and trunk.

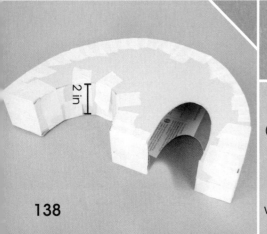

2 in

2 in

138

7.
Mix ¾ white glue with ¼ water in a bowl. Paste small sections of the mixture onto the elephant, sticking on strips of newspaper as you go. Brush another layer of glue over the top of the newspaper. Leave to dry.

8.
Use your elephant as a template to cut out two sheets of wrapping paper, but make them 1 in wider all around.

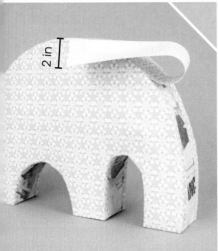

9.
Use the glue mixture to stick the wrapping paper over the newspaper. Cut small flaps into the excess edges of wrapping paper, 1 in apart, as shown. Then fold the flaps flat against the elephant and stick down with the all-purpose glue.

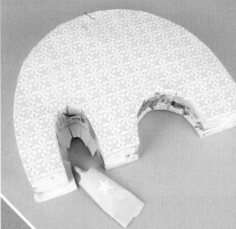

10.
Keep going until you've glued down all the flaps.

2 in

11.
Cut strips of wrapping paper, 2 in wide, and use the glue mixture to stick the paper over the top of the elephant and inside its trunk and legs.

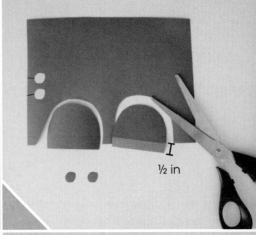

½ in

12.
Cut two semicircles from gray colored paper for the ears. Make a fold ½ in up from the bottom edge of each ear. Cut two small circles for eyes.

13.
Cut a tail shape from blue colored paper.

14.
Dab all-purpose glue onto the tail and along the folds of each ear, then stick them to the elephant. Repeat the steps to make another elephant bookend!

COOL IN CREPE!

PAPER
RA-RA
SKIRT

Make a nifty no-sew skirt! Simply cut out, fold, and glue your way to fashion fabulousness with this 1980s throwback skirt made from crepe paper!

* Caution: glue guns are hot, so ask an adult to help!

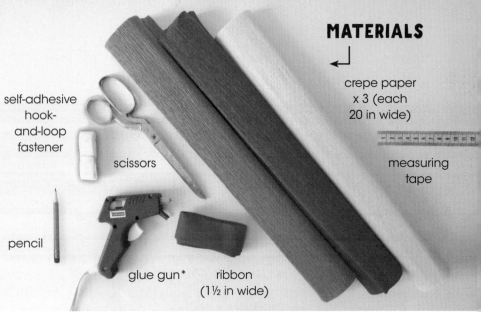

self-adhesive hook-and-loop fastener

scissors

pencil

glue gun*

ribbon (1½ in wide)

crepe paper x 3 (each 20 in wide)

measuring tape

1. Measure your waist, then cut a piece of ribbon to the same length as your waist measurement, plus an additional 8 in.

2. Cut each piece of crepe paper to the same length as the ribbon.

3. Draw a line 5½ in from the bottom edge of one sheet of crepe paper.

4. Fold the crepe paper up to the marked line.

141

5. Place a little bit of glue 2 in away from the bottom right-hand edge of the folded paper.

6. Now fold the paper lengthwise, making a pleat all the way up to the top of the paper. Press firmly at the bottom of the pleat, so it sticks to the glue.

7. Repeat steps 5 and 6, gluing and folding pleats all the way along the paper, until you reach the left-hand edge.

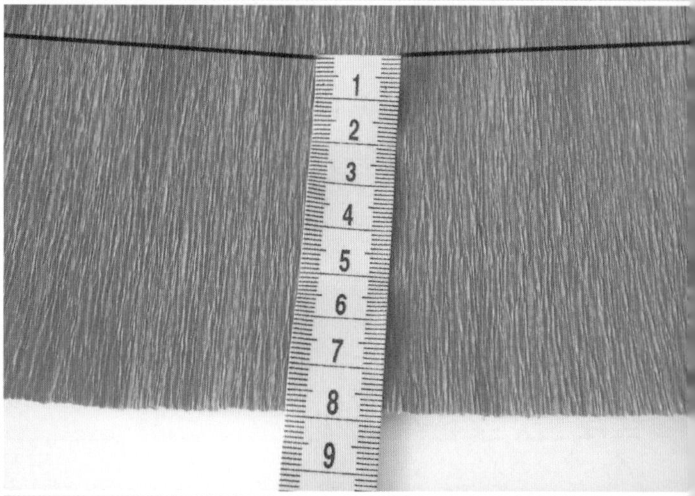

8. Now draw a line 3 in from the bottom edge of another sheet of crepe paper.

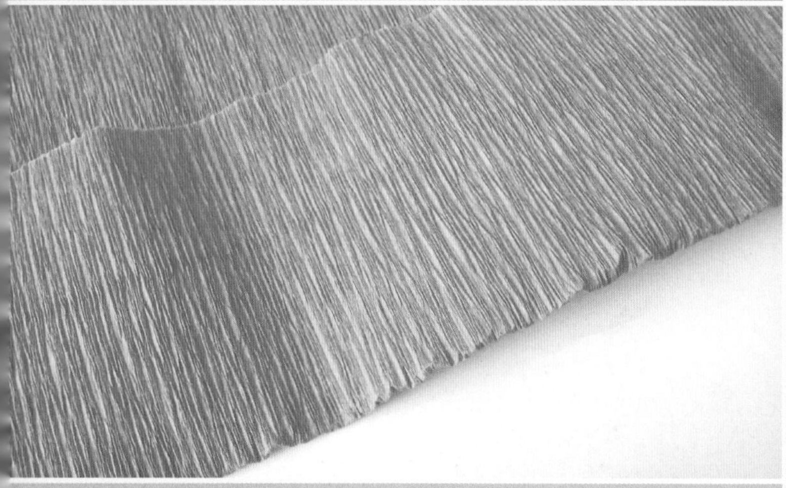

9. Fold the crepe paper up to the marked line.

10. Repeat steps 5 to 7 until this piece of crepe paper has also been pleated.

11. For the last piece of crepe paper, jump straight to steps 5 to 7, as it does not need to be folded at the bottom.

12. Now that all the pieces of paper have been pleated, lay them on top of each other, as shown. Glue them together along the top edges.

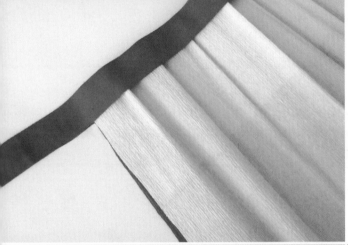

hook closure   loop closure

13. Now glue all the way along the ribbon, then place it over the top edge of the skirt. Line up the right-hand side of the ribbon with the right-hand side of the paper. Some ribbon will be left over on the left-hand side, as shown.

14. Turn the skirt over, then fold in half. Separate the hook-and-loop fastener. Glue the hook closure on top of the ribbon on the right-hand side of the skirt. Then add the loop closure to the underside of the ribbon (sticking out in the picture above).

15. Wrap the skirt around your waist, then join the hook-and-loop fastener together.

16. Wear leggings or shorts beneath your fab ra-ra skirt!

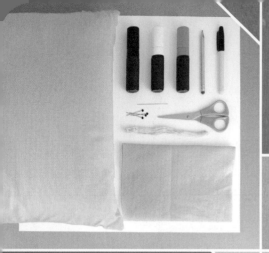

MATERIALS

square cream pillow (zip opening),
fabric pens (black, white, and orange),*
pencil, black marker, scissors, needle,
cream thread, cream felt, white cardstock
(similar size to pillow), sewing pins

* Follow the fabric pen instructions.

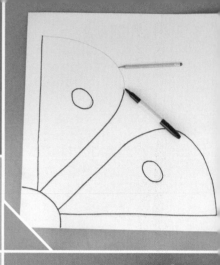

1.
Use a pencil to copy this fox picture
(right) onto the white cardstock. Then
draw over the lines with a marker.

2.
Remove the pillow from the pillow
cover and slide the white cardstock
inside. You should be able to see
your fox drawing through the pillow
cover. Trace over the design with
the fabric pens. Use the white pen
first, then the orange, and finish
with the black.

3.
Fold the cream felt in half and draw
a triangular ear shape, as shown.

4.
Keeping the felt folded, cut out the
ear shape. You will now have two
symmetrical fox ears.

5.
Use the fabric pens to create the
ear design (right). Wait for the
fabric pens to dry before moving
on to the next step.

6.
Roughly figure out where you want
the ears to be, then pin them in place
on the back of the pillow cover. Sew
on the ears with two rows of simple
running stitches.

7.
Remove the cardstock template and
slide the pillow back inside the
pillow cover. So cute!

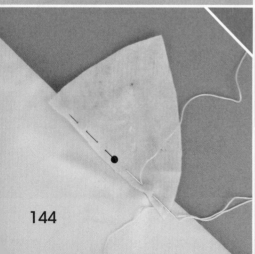

FACE-THE-FOX PILLOW

HELP!

RAIN
CLOUD
MOBILE

DRIP!
DROP!

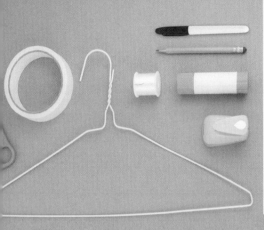

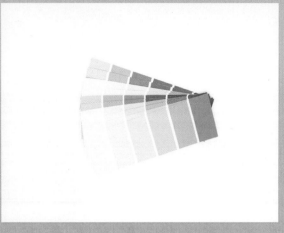

scissors,
masking tape,
wire coat hanger,
invisible thread,
pencil,
black marker,
glue stick,
raindrop hole punch
(optional),
white cardstock
(11 in x 17 in),
blue paint swatches

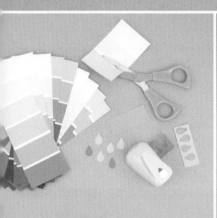

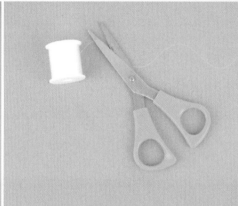

1. Cut the swatches into strips, then use the hole punch (or scissors) to create around 100 raindrops.

2. Place the wire coat hanger over the white cardstock. Sketch a cloud shape around the hanger, making it a little bigger than the hanger itself. Draw a face onto the cloud with the marker, then cut out the cloud shape.

3. Cut seven pieces of invisible thread (28 in each). Lay them on a work surface and stick masking tape at both ends of the pieces to hold in place.

4. Add glue to the back of a raindrop shape. Place the raindrop under the thread, then glue another raindrop over the top, sandwiching the thread between the two raindrops.

5. Continue to add more raindrops to each piece of invisible thread, placing them evenly apart. Use masking tape to attach each line of raindrops to the back of the cloud, as shown.

6. Stick the wire coat hanger to the cloud with long strips of masking tape. Now you're ready to hang up your super-cool rain cloud mobile.

MATERIALS

shrink plastic*,
black marker,
ruler,
scissors,
keyring,
baking sheet,
waxed paper,
heavy book

*Follow the shrink plastic instructions.

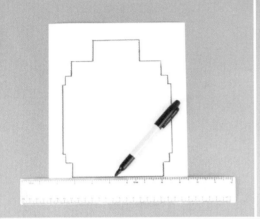

1. Using your ruler and marker, draw a geometric shape on the shrink plastic.

2. Create a geometric pattern inside the outline, still using your ruler.

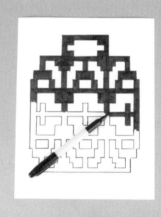

3. Color areas of the pattern with your pen.

4. Cut out the shape, leaving a ¼-in border around the edges, as shown. Cut a hole big enough to fit over your keyring once shrunk.

5. Place your design on a piece of waxed paper on a baking sheet. Read the instructions for the shrink plastic, and put it in the oven.*

*Ask an adult to do this for you.

6. When your design has shrunk, take the baking sheet out of the oven* and press a heavy book over the design. When cool, add a keyring through the hole.

*Ask an adult to do this for you.

IT'S GEO-NIUS!

MELTED CRAYON MASTERPIECE

MATERIALS

40 to 50 crayons
foam board (11 in x 17 in)
black construction paper
pencil
scissors
glue stick
glue gun*
hair dryer*

1. Draw a person holding an umbrella on black paper and cut out the shape. Now glue into place on the bottom left-hand corner of the foam board, 2 in away from the side.

2. Glue the crayons across the top of the foam board with the glue gun, as shown.*

* Ask an adult to do this step for you.

3. Put something behind the foam board so it stands up at a slight angle. Then turn on your hair dryer and point it at the first few crayons until they melt. Now point your hair dryer at the next few, and so on, until all the crayons have melted.**

* Caution: glue guns are hot, so ask an adult to help!
** Do not touch the crayons, or the end of the hair dryer, until cooled.

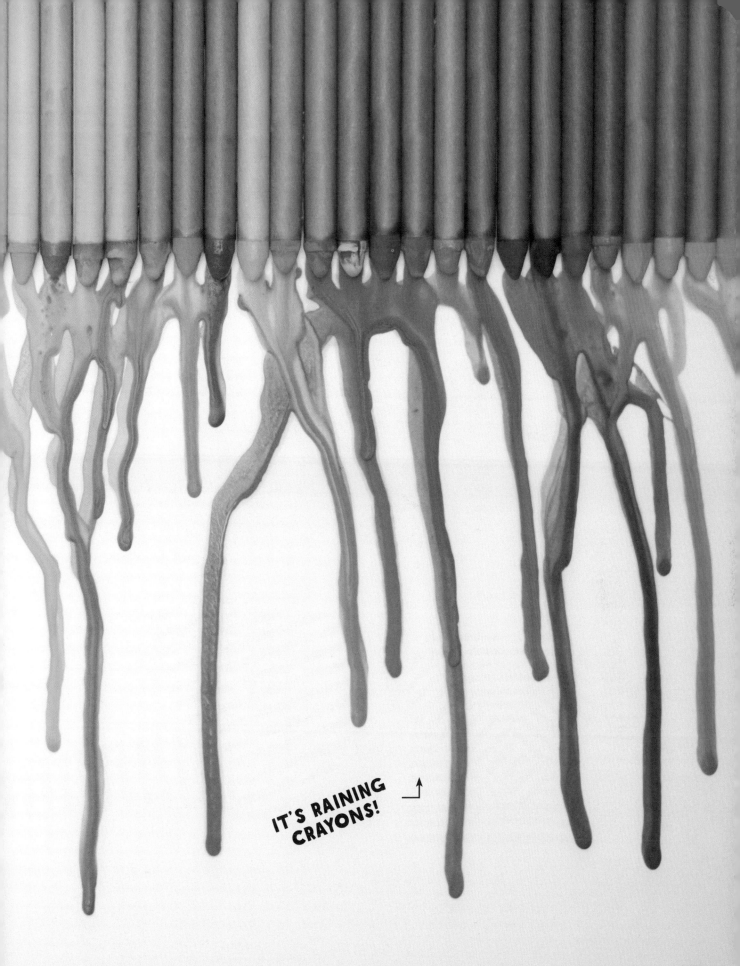

IT'S RAINING CRAYONS!

TOP-DOG
DRAFT STOPPER

MATERIALS

long-sleeved striped top, red felt, toy stuffing, needle, buttons x 2, pencil, pins, scissors, red and blue embroidery thread

1. Turn the top inside out and position it to match the above picture. Draw the shape of a dog's head on the body of the top, joining it to the arm (as shown). Pin both sides of the top together just inside the pencil line.

WOOF!

WOOF!

2. Carefully cut out the dog's head, following the pencil line as shown.

3. Line up the other sleeve alongside the one that has just been cut out. Cut off the second sleeve, just beneath the dog's head on the first sleeve. Use the stripes to guide you. Now cut off both cuffs where the sleeves start to narrow.

4. Turn the second sleeve inside out and push it inside the arm of the first sleeve (the one with the dog's head). Line up the sleeve ends.

5. Pin the sleeves together through the first two layers of fabric around the entire sleeve circumference. Sew a stretch stitch just inside the pinned lines (but don't sew the sleeves closed). Remove the pins.

6. Now stretch stitch just inside the pins around the head shape. Remove the pins.

7. Turn your dog the right way out (the second sleeve added in step 4 will also be pulled out). Fill the dog with the toy stuffing.

8. Leave 6 in from the end unstuffed for the tail. Squeeze the fabric together, as shown.

9. Tie a knot as close as possible to the stuffing.

10. Fold the piece of felt in half and draw three rectangles with rounded ends along the folded edge.

11. Carefully cut out each rectangle.

12. Unfold two pieces of felt, and place at both ends of the body for legs, as shown. Pin the legs in place, then sew a running stitch along the center of each felt piece to attach them.

13. Cut the remaining piece of felt in half (along the fold) to make a pair of ears.

14. Pin an ear to each side of the dog's head. Sew each ear on with a running stitch at the top. Remove the pins.

15. Now sew the button eyes on each side of the head. What a paw-fect pooch!

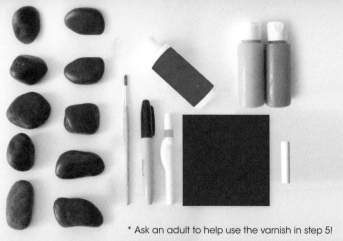

* Ask an adult to help use the varnish in step 5!

MATERIALS

pebbles x 10, paintbrush, black marker, acrylic paints, correction fluid, clear varnish, * black paper, chalk

1. Paint five blue pebbles, then five orange pebbles, using acrylic paint. Leave to dry.

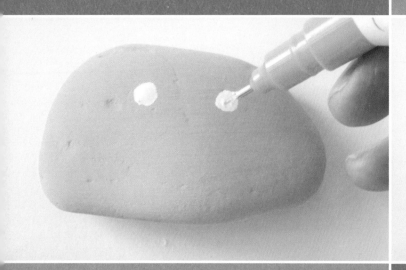

2. To create a monster face, blob two eyes on a blue pebble with correction fluid. Leave to dry.

3. Add the pupils and mouth with the marker. Then paint some gappy teeth with the correction fuid.

4. Create different funny monster faces on the remaining nine pebbles, as shown.

5. Varnish the pebbles for protection, then draw a gr of 9 squares on black paper with chalk. Play with friend, choosing to be either blue or orange. Take turns placing your pebbles on the grid. The first to get three same-colored pebbles in a row wins!

TIC-TAC-OHHHH!

MAKE A MONSTER MOVE WITH THESE SPOOKY PEBBLES!

PEN-CHANTING PATTERNS

Customize your things with some simple pen designs.
Stamp your style on caps, lunch boxes, or whatever you like!

Upcycle a plain glass into a work of art with a glass pen. Why not add a stray square in a spotty pattern and see if your friends can find it!?

Fabric pens are a fab way to customize clothes. Experiment with different patterns, and maybe add a twist. Can you spot the rebellious arrow in this design?

Create a simple crosshatch patterned lunch box with a permanent marker.

Ballpoint pens are a terrific doodle tool for stationery. Try different doodly designs on folders, notepads, and diaries.

Give a dark frame a super-snazzy pattern using white correction fluid!

Storage boxes don't have to be boring! Bring yours to life with a chalk marker and some triangular patterns.

Metallic markers are great for giving a shimmery finish, like on this patterned pencil case.

EYE SPOT A PEACOCK

FANCY TAIL!

MATERIALS

scissors,
black pen,
all-purpose glue,
patterned fabric scraps,
stretched plain canvas,
white cardstock (half the
size of the canvas),
craft foam (same size as
the white cardstock)

↵

* Ask an adult to help use the all-purpose
glue in steps 3 and 4!

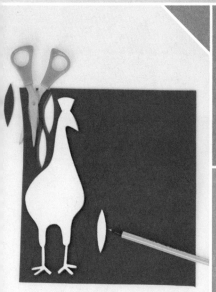

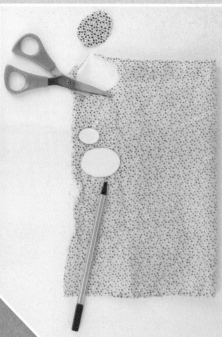

1.
Draw a peacock body and leaf shape for feathers onto a sheet of cardstock and cut out as templates for this craft. Use the template to draw the peacock body and 14 leaf feathers onto a sheet of foam. Then cut them out.

2.
Draw a larger and smaller oval onto the sheet of cardstock and cut out as a template for the eye feathers on the peacock. Now use these templates to create 13 large eye feathers and 26 small eye feathers from the different types of patterned fabric.

3.
Next glue the peacock body to the middle of the canvas. Add some large and small eye feathers around it.

4.
Glue some of the small eye feathers in the middle of the larger ones. Now add the leaf feathers around the outside to finish. What a pretty peacock!

COOL CARDBOARD CASTLE

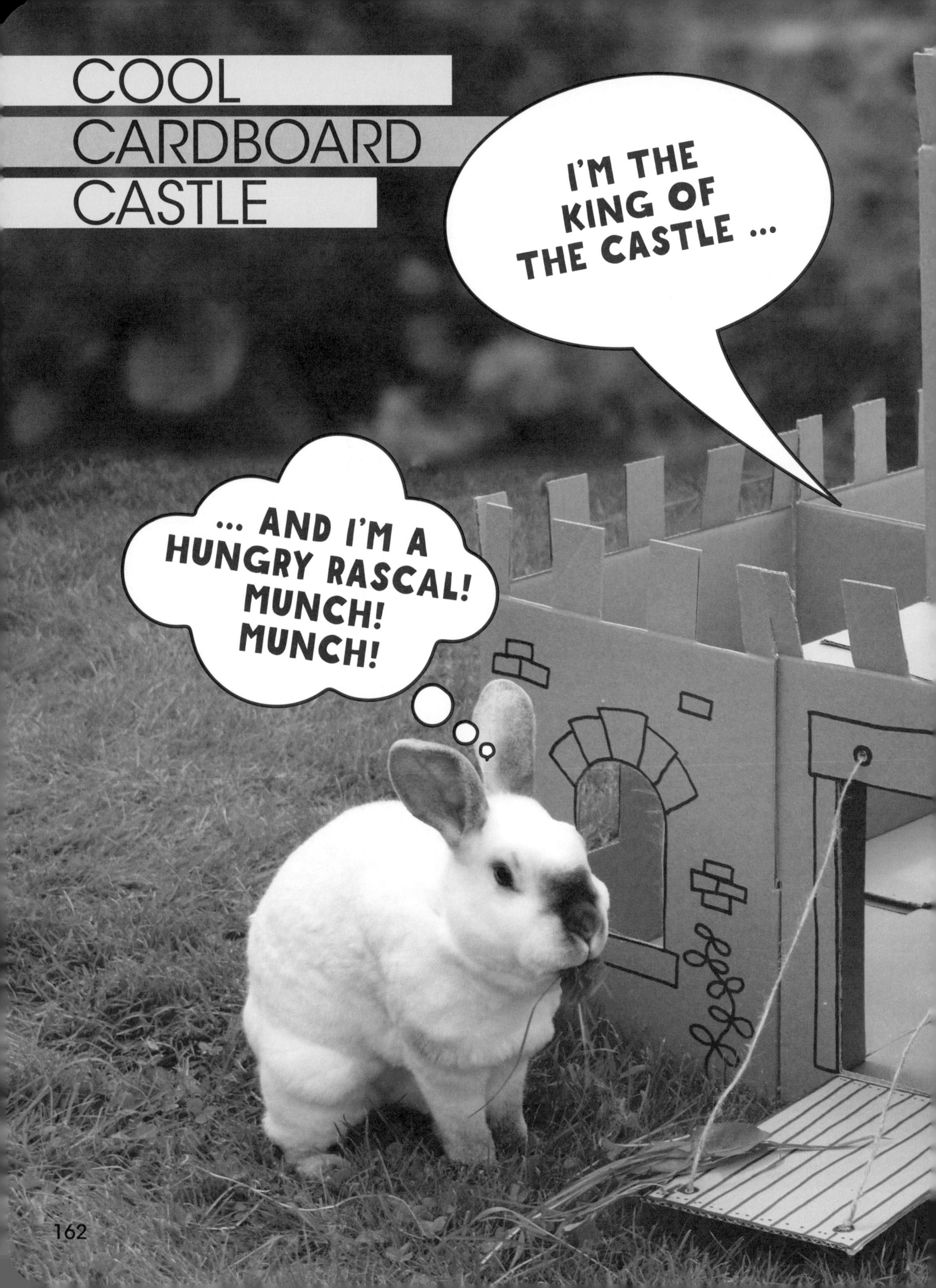

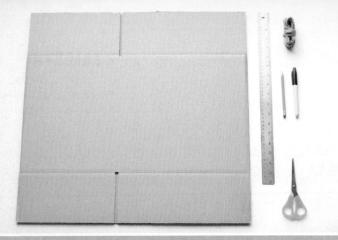

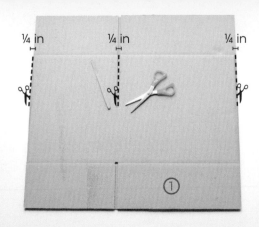

MATERIALS

flat-packed cardboard boxes x 7 (12 in x 9 in x 10 in), ruler, pencil, scissors, twine, black marker

1. Label the boxes 1 to 7 in pencil. Take box 1 and cut three ¼ in wide slots (from top to middle), as shown.

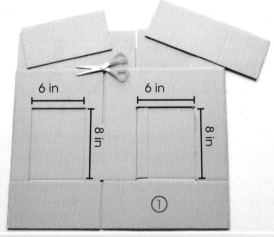

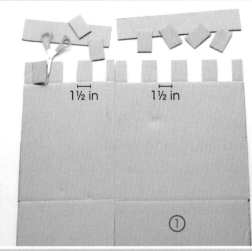

2. Draw two doorways, one on each side of the box (6 in x 8 in), then carefully cut them out. Cut off the two top flaps.

3. Turn over the box. Draw battlements (1½ in wide) on the two top flaps, then cut them out.

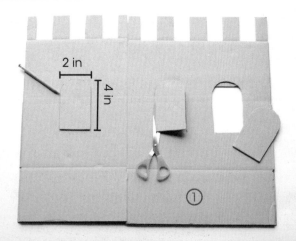

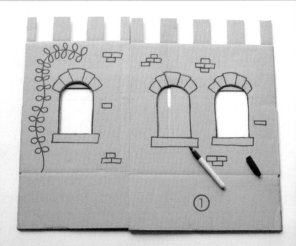

4. Use some of the waste cardboard to make a window template (4 in x 2 in) with a rounded top, then cut it out. Use your template to draw three windows on the two sides of the box facing upward, then carefully cut them out.

5. Add detail on the two sides of the box, such as ivy and bricks, with your pen.

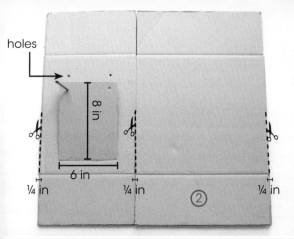

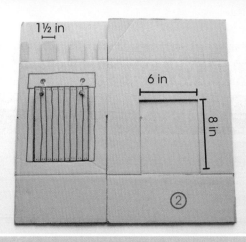

6. Take box 2 and cut three ¼ in wide slots (from bottom to middle), as shown. Draw a drawbridge on the left side of the box (6 in x 8 in), then cut out the top and sides, and fold down the bottom. Make four holes on the cardboard, as shown.

7. Thread two pieces of twine (each 12 in long) through the holes to make the drawbridge chains. Tie knots at either end. Create a doorway on the right side of the box and battlements on the left top flap. Add detail with your pen.

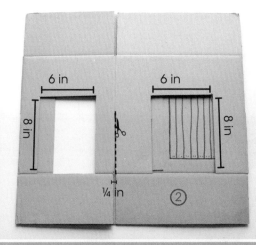

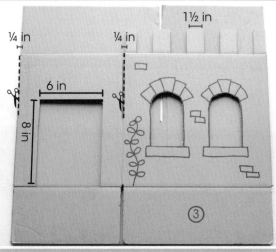

8. Turn over the box and cut a ¼ in wide slot (from bottom to middle), as shown. Create two doorways, one on each side of the box.

9. Take box 3 and cut two ¼ in wide slots (from top to middle), as shown. Create a doorway on the left side of the box, then cut off the left top flap. Create battlements on the right top flap and two windows on the right side of the box. Add detail with your pen.

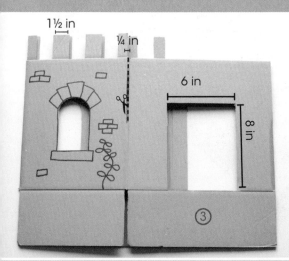

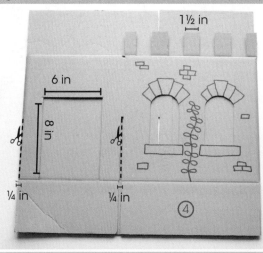

10. Turn over the box and cut a ¼ in wide slot (from top to middle), as shown. Create battlements on the left top flap and a window on the left side of the box. Create a doorway on the right side of the box, then cut off the right top flap. Add detail.

11. Take box 4 and cut two ¼ in wide slots (from bottom to middle), as shown. Create a doorway on the left side of the box, then cut off the left top flap. Create battlements on the right top flap and two windows on the right side of the box. Add detail.

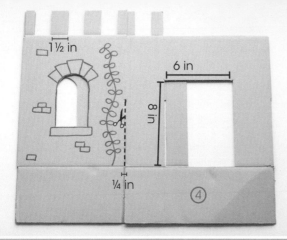

12. Turn over the box and cut a ¼ in wide slot (from bottom to middle), as shown. Create battlements on the left top flap and a window on the left side of the box. Create a doorway on the right side of the box, then cut off the right top flap. Add detail.

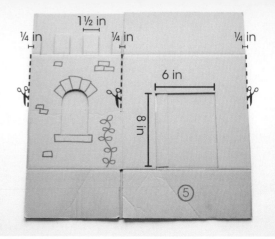

13. Take box 5 and cut three ¼ in wide slots (from top to middle), as shown. Create battlements on the left top flap and a window on the left side of the box. Create a doorway on the right side of the box. Add detail.

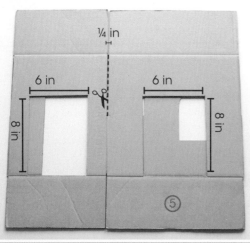

14. Turn over the box and cut a ¼ in wide slot (from top to middle), as shown. Create two doorways, one on each side of the box.

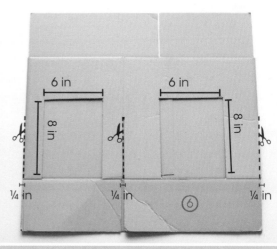

15. Take box 6 and cut three ¼ in wide slots (from bottom to middle), as shown. Create two doorways, one on each side of the box, then cut off the two top flaps.

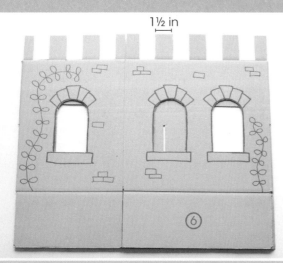

16. Turn over the box. Create battlements on the two top flaps and three windows on the two sides of the box. Add detail.

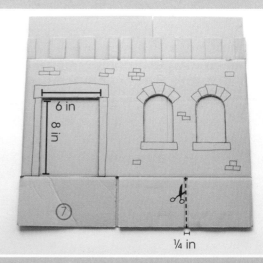

17. Take box 7 and cut a ¼ in wide slot (from bottom fold line) halfway across the width of the right bottom flap, as shown. Create a doorway on the left side of the box, battlements on the two top flaps, and two windows on the right side of the box. Add detail.

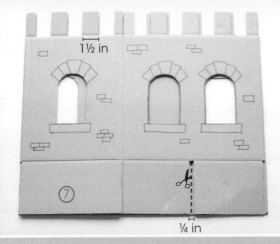

18. Turn over the box and cut a ¼ in wide slot (from bottom to fold line) halfway across the width of the right bottom flap, as shown. Create battlements on the two top flaps and three windows on the two sides of the box. Add detail.

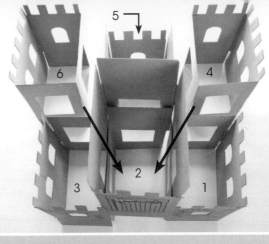

19. Stand boxes 1 to 6 in the order shown. Make sure the decorated sides face out. Lift box 2 above the others and slide it into the slots of boxes 1, 3, and 5. Carefully push box 2 down so the slots interlock and it becomes level with the other boxes.

20. Lift box 4 above the others and slide it into the slots of boxes 1 and 5. Push box 4 down so the slots interlock. Now slide box 6 into the slots of boxes 3 and 5. Push box 6 down so the slots interlock.

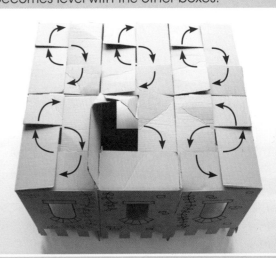

21. Turn the castle upside down, carefully resting the battlements on the floor. Interlock the flaps on the base of each box, as shown.

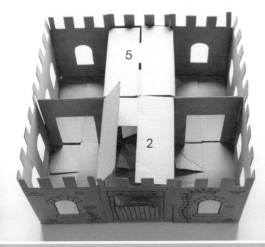

22. Turn the castle the right way around, and fold the top flaps of boxes 2 and 5 inward to form another floor.

23. Lift box 7 above the "floor" and slide the longer bottom flaps into boxes 1 and 4 (on one side), and 3 and 6 (on the other). Lay the smaller bottom flaps on the "floor"!

167

MATERIALS

pair of gloves, needle, thread, scissors, toy stuffing, big white buttons x 2, small colored buttons x 2, black marker

1.

Turn the gloves inside out, then draw a curved line at the top of each glove to make a rough body shape, as shown.

2.

Carefully cut along the curved lines.

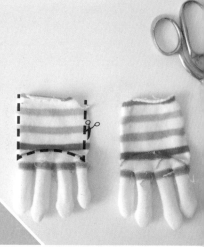

3.

Draw another curved line ¾ in up from the fingers of each glove. Remove the top "layer" of each glove by cutting the side seams down and along each line. Both gloves should now have one long layer and one short layer.

4.

Using a running stitch, sew the gloves together (with the shorter layers on the inside). Sew around the edges, starting and ending just above the fingers.

5.

Open out the gloves, as shown. Sew together the section between the fingers with a running stitch. Leave a ¾-in gap at one end for the stuffing.

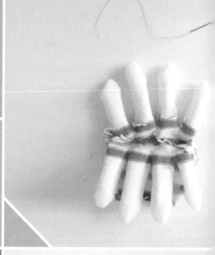

6.

Turn the gloves inside out so the stitching is hidden. Fill your octopus with stuffing, then close up the gap from step 5 using a running stitch.

7.

To finish, sew on some button eyes. Stitch the big white buttons on first, then add the small colored buttons on top.

I GLOVE YOU!

GLOVE-LY OCTOPUS

169

MATERIALS

strips of colored paper, picture frame, cardstock (to fit inside frame), quilling tool, pencil, black marker, white glue, plate

1.

First turn the strips of paper into spirals. Slot the end of one piece of paper into the quilling tool, then twirl it around.

2.

When the entire strip of paper has been curled into a tight roll, carefully remove it from the quilling tool.

3.

Dab some glue on the end of the spiral to stick it together, then leave to dry. Continue making quilled spirals until you have about 60 or 70 altogether.

4.

Draw a circle for the hot-air balloon and a small basket below onto some cardstock. Draw lines to attach the basket to the balloon and add a character in the basket!

5.

Use the pen to draw over everything except the balloon. Sketch some clouds with the pen, to give your picture extra detail.

6.

Pour some glue onto a plate, then dip the edge of a spiral into the glue. Now glue the spiral onto the balloon shape, as shown.

7.

Continue adding more spirals until the balloon is completely covered. Leave to dry, then frame your hot-air balloon picture and hang it up!*

* Ask an adult to help.

GET HOOKED
ON CROCHET
WITH THIS
WOOLLY GADGET!

COZY CROCHET TABLET CASE

MATERIALS

sewing machine, fabric x 2, wadding, yarn, crochet hook, scissors, needle, thread, pins, button

1.
To make a slip knot, create a loop in the yarn, as shown. Insert the hook through the loop and hook under the tail. Pull the tail to tighten the yarn around the hook, creating a loop on the hook.

2.
To make a chain stitch, bring the yarn over the hook (from back to front) and hook it. Draw the hooked yarn through the loop on the hook.

3.
Repeat step 2 five more times, to make 6 chain stitches in total.

4.
To make a slip stitch (in order to create a ring), insert the hook through the first chain stitch, then bring the yarn over the hook (from back to front) and hook it. Draw the hooked yarn through both the stitch and the loop on the hook.

5.
Repeat step 2 three times to make 3 chain stitches in total.

6.
To make a double crochet stitch, bring the yarn over the hook (from back to front), then insert the hook through the center of the ring. Bring the yarn over the hook (from back to front) and hook it.

7.
Pull the hook back through the center of the ring. You should now have three loops on the hook.

8.
Now bring the yarn over the hook (from back to front) and hook it. Draw the hooked yarn through two loops on the hook. You should now have two loops on the hook.

9.
Now bring the yarn over the hook (from back to front) and hook it. Draw the hooked yarn through both loops on the hook. You've finished your double crochet stitch!

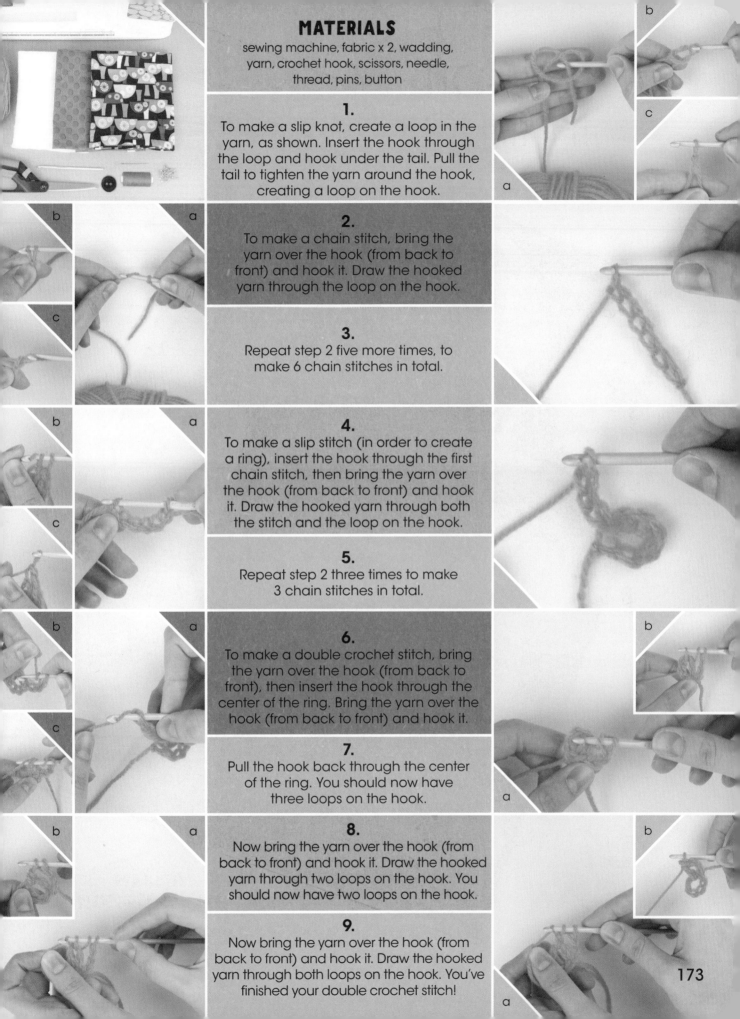

10.
Repeat steps 6 to 9 ten times to make 11 double crochet stitches in total.

11.
To finish this row, make a slip stitch through the top of the 3 chain stitches (see step 4).

b

c

a

12.
Now you're ready to start the second row! First, repeat step 2 three times to make 3 chain stitches in total.

13.
Repeat steps 6 to 9 twice to make 2 double crochet stitches in the first gap in the row below. Then repeat step 2 to make 1 chain stitch.

b

a

14.
Repeat step 13 to make 11 more sets of 2 double crochet stitches followed by 1 chain stitch.

15.
To finish this row, make a slip stitch through the top of the 3 chain stitches (see step 4).

b

a

16.
Now you're ready to start the third row! First, repeat step 2 three times to make 3 chain stitches in total.

17.
Repeat steps 6 to 9 twice to make 2 double crochet stitches in the first gap (between each pair of double crochet stitches) in the row below. Then repeat step 2 twice to make 2 chain stitches.

18.
Repeat step 17 to make 11 more sets of 2 double crochet stitches followed by 2 chain stitches.

19.
To finish this row, make a slip stitch through the top of the 3 chain stitches (see step 4).

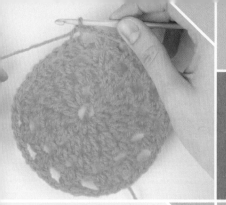

20.
Now you're ready to start the fourth and final row! Follow steps 16 to 19.

21.
To cast off, pull the loop on the hook (making it bigger). Remove the hook. Cut off the yarn, then feed the end (or tail) through the loop, and pull tight. Use a needle to guide the two tails of yarn through your work a few times.

22.
For the case, fold a piece of fabric in half (at the bottom), then lay the tablet on top. Cut the fabric, making it ¾ in larger all around than the case.

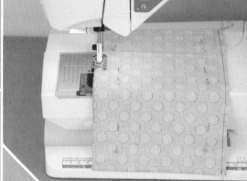

23.
Turn the fabric inside out (still folded). Pin the two long sides together and sew straight stitches down each one (¼ in from the edge).

24.
Follow steps 22 and 23 with the other fabric. Then cut out two pieces of wadding the same size as your tablet.

25.
Turn the two fabric pieces the right way around, then slide a piece of wadding inside each one.

26.
Now pin the two fabric pieces together, making sure the unsewn ends line up. Sew the unsewn end and the two longer sides of the case (¼ in from the edge), leaving the other shorter end unsewn.

27.
Turn the case right side out, so the seams are on the inside. Check to be sure your tablet fits snugly inside.

28.
At the opening of the case, place half of your crochet circle over the top, as shown. Use a needle and thread to sew a simple running stitch from the crochet circle to the first fabric layer of your case.

29.
Stitch a button on the other side, then pop it through the crochet lid to close.

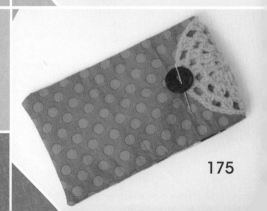

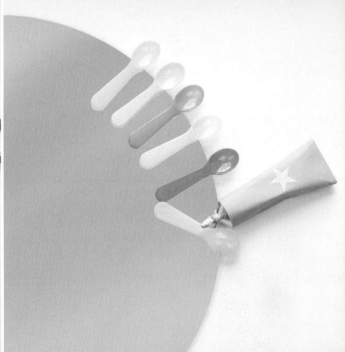

MATERIALS
circular acrylic mirror, plastic spoons, all-purpose glue*

* Ask an adult to help use the all-purpose glue in each step!

1. Add a few drops of glue to the back of a spoon, then glue it onto the edge of the mirror. Keep adding more spoons, spacing them ½ in apart from each other.

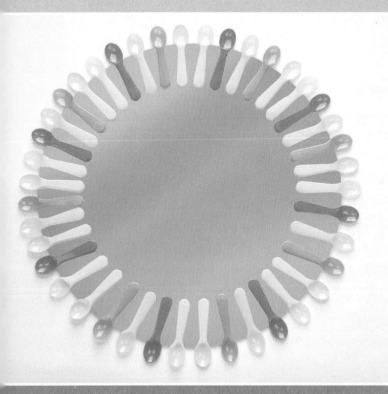

2. Continue gluing the spoons all around the mirror, alternating the colors as you go!

3. Now add a second layer of spoons, gluing them in the gaps from the first row. Continue until the outer edge of the mirror is hidden by spoons. When you've finished, hang it up!*

* Ask an adult to help

SUPER SPOON MIRROR

MIRROR, MIRROR ON THE WALL, WE'RE THE FAIREST SPOONS OF ALL!

CRANE ORIG-ARMY

FOLD A FLOCK OF PRETTY BIRDS!

1.
a. Fold the paper diagonally in half
from top right to bottom left corner.
b. Now fold in half again,
from top left to bottom right.

2.
Fold the bottom right-hand corner
of the top flap of the triangle
across to the left.

3.
a. Open up and spread the top flap
out from the inside.
b. Fold it flat to make a square.

4.
Flip the paper over from right to left.
Fold the bottom left-hand corner
across to the right.
a. Open up and spread the new flap
out from the inside.
b. Fold it flat to make a square.

5.
a. Rotate the square 45° clockwise,
so the square looks like a diamond.
Then fold the right and left sides
into the center.
b. Press the creases flat.

6.
a. Fold the top corner down to the
dotted line.
b. Now unfold the folds made in
steps 5 and 6a.

7.
a. Open the pocket by pulling the
top layer of paper from the bottom
of the diamond (point 1) up.
b. Points 2 and 3 should fold into
the center. Press flat to make
an elongated diamond.

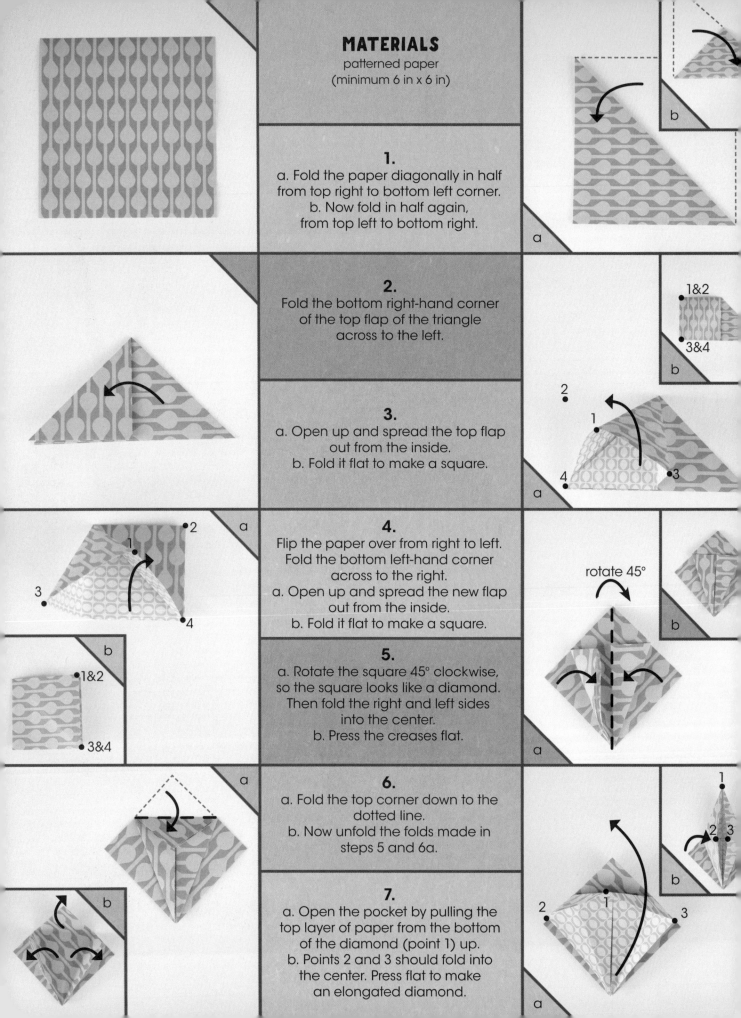

8.
Flip the paper over from right to left and repeat steps 5 to 7 on this side. However, there is no need to rotate the square 45°.

9.
a. Fold the right and left sides into the center.
b. Press the creases flat.

b

a

10.
Flip the paper over from right to left and repeat step 9 on this side.

11.
a. Fold the right point up to the dashed line. Then unfold.
b. Now separate the two layers of the right point. Guide the point up inside the two layers of paper.
c. Press the point flat at the crease. The right point should now be sandwiched between two layers of the body.

right point

b

body

right point

a

c

12.
Repeat step 11 for the left point.

13.
Fold the tip of the right point down, so that you form the beak.

14.
a. To make the wings, fold the top layer of the center point down to reveal the body, and fold.
b. Now flip it over and repeat on the other side.

a

b

15.
To finish, spread the wings out by pulling them slightly away from each other. Make as many cranes as you like, then chain them together on a string!

STAMP
IT
OUT!

FABU-MASH PINEAPPLE PRINT

MATERIALS

paper plates,
fabric paints*,
old T-shirt,
potato masher,
fork

* Follow the fabric paint instructions.

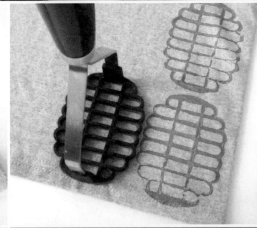

1. Squeeze some fabric paint onto a paper plate. Place the potato masher in the paint, then spread it around to get an even coverage.

2. Now line up the masher with the bottom of the T-shirt and press down firmly.

3. Apply more paint to the masher before making a new stamp on the T-shirt. Then try adding different colors to your design. With each new color, first rinse out the masher with water.

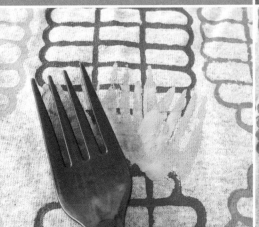

4. Take your fork and press the prongs into the fabric paint, making sure to cover the fork evenly.

5. Press the fork head to the top of each pineapple three times (to create a row). This makes the leaf detail.

6. Keep stamping until you're happy with your T-shirt design. Tee-rrific!

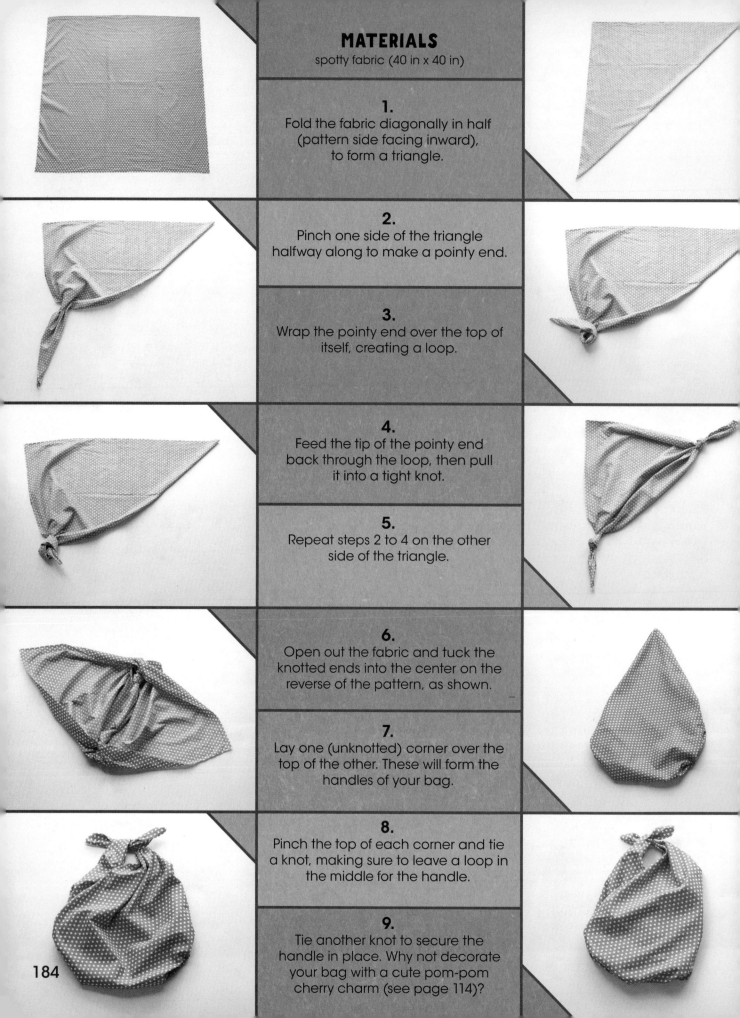

MATERIALS

spotty fabric (40 in x 40 in)

1.
Fold the fabric diagonally in half (pattern side facing inward), to form a triangle.

2.
Pinch one side of the triangle halfway along to make a pointy end.

3.
Wrap the pointy end over the top of itself, creating a loop.

4.
Feed the tip of the pointy end back through the loop, then pull it into a tight knot.

5.
Repeat steps 2 to 4 on the other side of the triangle.

6.
Open out the fabric and tuck the knotted ends into the center on the reverse of the pattern, as shown.

7.
Lay one (unknotted) corner over the top of the other. These will form the handles of your bag.

8.
Pinch the top of each corner and tie a knot, making sure to leave a loop in the middle for the handle.

9.
Tie another knot to secure the handle in place. Why not decorate your bag with a cute pom-pom cherry charm (see page 114)?

WHAT'S KNOT
TO LIKE?

SPOTTY
KNOTTY
BAG

Once upon a time, Little Red Riding Hood set off through the woods to visit her sick grandmother. Along the way, she met a BIG BAD WOLF and ... well, you know the rest! Try making these simple spoon puppets, then put on your very own fairy-tale puppet show.

MATERIALS

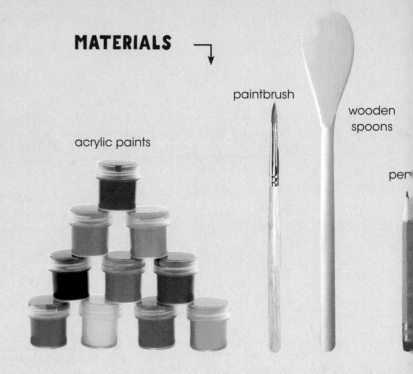

acrylic paints

paintbrush

wooden spoons

pen

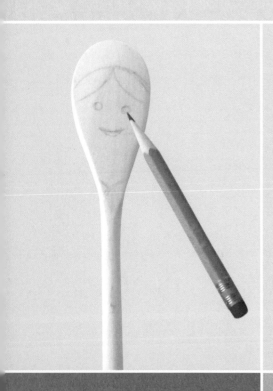

1. Draw Little Red Riding Hood's face and hood on a spoon, as shown. Sketch some lines for her cape.

2. Now paint the red hood and cape, then leave to dry.

3. Paint Little Red Riding Hood's black hair, features, and bow. Then turn more spoons into her grandmother, the hunter, and the Big Bad Wolf

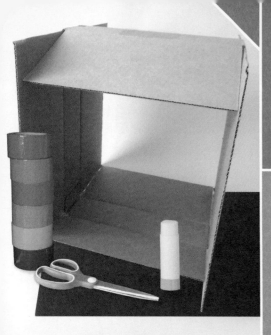

MATERIALS
unfolded cardboard box,
several different-colored rolls of duct tape,
scissors, black paper, glue stick

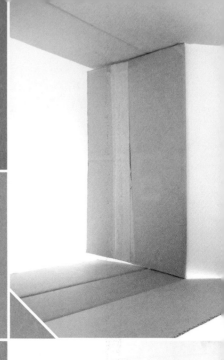

1.
Lay the box on its side. Tape the two side flaps to the walls inside. This is so you can easily move your puppets around the theater when it's finished.

2.
Fold the bottom flap upward and tape it in place, as shown. Fold the top flap upward, but leave untaped.

3.
Using the duct tape, decorate the front of the box in colorful stripes.

4.
Continue adding the striped pattern around the outside and the inside of the box. This will create colorful edges at the front of the box.

5.
Finally, glue black paper to the insides of the box, as well as the top flap. This will give your theater a professional finish. Draw a picture of some scenery for the backdrop, and it's showtime!

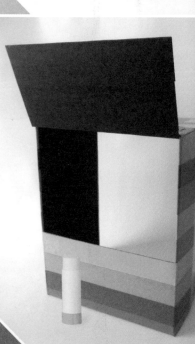

PUPPET
SHOW!

TODAY AT 3PM

HE'S BEHIND
YOU!

PRETTY BEAD SUNCATCHER

MAKE 'EM
MELT!

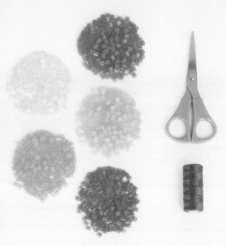

MATERIALS
aluminum foil,
cookie sheet,
springform cake ring,
star-shaped cookie cutters x 3,
round cookie cutters x 3,
small, fusible plastic beads*,
scissors,
thread

* Beads must be suitable for craft making and for use with an iron or oven!

1.
Preheat the oven to 400°F.* Now line a cookie sheet with foil and place the star-shaped cookie cutters on top. Fill the cutters with beads.
* Ask an adult to do this for you.

2.
Put the cookie sheet in the oven for 10 minutes, and then remove.*
* Ask an adult to do this for you.

3.
Once cooled, remove the cutters from the star-shaped beads. Place the large cake ring inside the cookie sheet and around the stars. Add more colored beads inside the ring, as shown, and repeat step 2.

4.
To make the smaller circles, follow steps 1 to 2, but use the round cookie cutters.

5.
Feed a piece of thread through the top of each bead circle. Now tie the bead shapes together (using a double knot), as shown. Hang your pretty suncatcher outside or in a window!

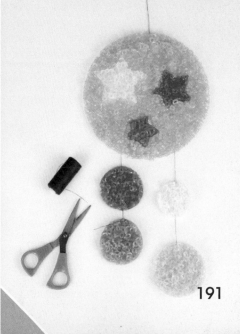

191

COMIC STRIP TABLETOP

MATERIALS
old comics, books, or magazines
old, small table*
scissors
white glue
water
bowl
paintbrush

* Check with an adult first before using!

1. Mix ¾ white glue with ¼ water in a bowl.

2. Cut out pictures from the comics, books, or magazines.

3. Paint a thin layer of the glue mixture onto a small area of the table, then stick on some of the cutouts.

4. Repeat step 3 until the entire table is covered with cutouts. Leave to dry.

5. To finish, brush another layer of glue mixture over the table to seal your design. Once dry, it's ready to use!

KA-POW!

MATERIALS

strips of patterned paper,
old book,
butterfly hole punch
(optional),
adhesive putty,
glue stick,
scissors (optional)

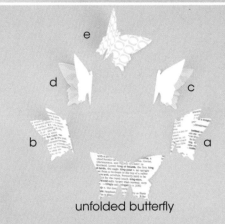

unfolded butterfly

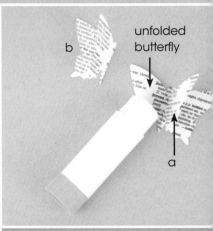

unfolded butterfly

1. Use the butterfly hole punch (or scissors) to create lots of butterfly shapes from the patterned paper and torn-out pages from the old book.

2. Take six butterflies. Fold five of them in half, as shown, *a* to *e*. Make sure the patterned (or printed) paper is on the inside.

3. Add glue to the wings of the unfolded butterfly. Press folded butterfly *a* onto the right side of the unfolded butterfly, matching the wing shapes together. Then press folded butterfly *b* onto the left side of the unfolded butterfly.

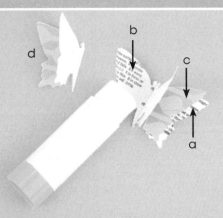

4. Add glue to the outer wings of butterflies *a* and *b*. Press butterfly *c* on top of *a* (on the right side), and butterfly *d* on top of *b* (on the left side).

5. Unfold butterfly *e*. Stick it on top of the outer wings of butterflies *c* and *d*, pattern side facing out.

6. Carefully fan out each wing give your butterfly a 3D look. Add some adhesive putty to back of the butterfly and att it to a wall. Repeat steps 2 to 6 until you have lots of pretty fluttering butterflies.

FLUTTERING BUTTERFLIES

DON'T WORRY, BE FLAPPY!

PINCUSHION CACTUS

OUCH!

IT'S PRICKLY!

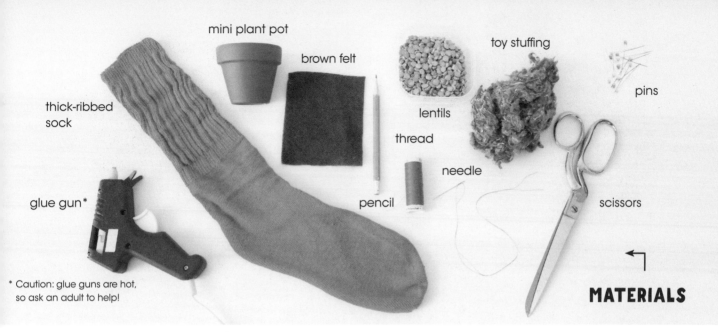

mini plant pot

brown felt

toy stuffing

pins

thick-ribbed
sock

lentils

thread

needle

scissors

pencil

glue gun*

* Caution: glue guns are hot,
so ask an adult to help!

MATERIALS

¾ in
(non-ribbed pattern)

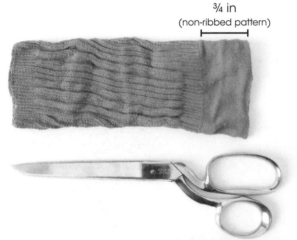

1. Cut off the foot of the sock, leaving ¾ in of non-ribbed pattern at the end.

2. Fold the sock in half lengthwise. Sew the two sides together with a running stitch, leaving the ends unstitched.

3. Now sew the top of the sock closed. First stitch together the inner layer, as shown, gathering all the stitches into a point.

4. Repeat step 3 for the outer layer of the sock.

197

5. Flip the sock inside out (push a pencil inside to help, if needed).

6. Fill the sock evenly with stuffing, then set aside.

7. To create the "soil," place the pot upside down on the brown felt, and trace around it.

8. Use your scissors to cut out the circle.

9. Fold the circle in half and make a ½-in snip in the middle. Fold in half the other way and repeat.

10. The felt should now have two slots forming a cross, as shown.

11. Insert the bottom (unstitched) section of the sock through the felt.

12. Now add a good amount of glue in the bottom of the pot.*

* Ask an adult to do this for you.

13. Firmly press the unstitched end of the sock into the glue.

14. Fill the pot with dried lentils to prevent the cactus from tipping over.

15. Glue all around the inner edge of the pot,* then stick the edges of brown felt over the glue.

* Ask an adult to do this for you.

16. Now push your pins into the sock to complete your pincushion cactus. Spiky!

199

MATERIALS

plain file box,
used postage stamps,
pencil,
scissors,
glue stick,
white vinyl sticky paper

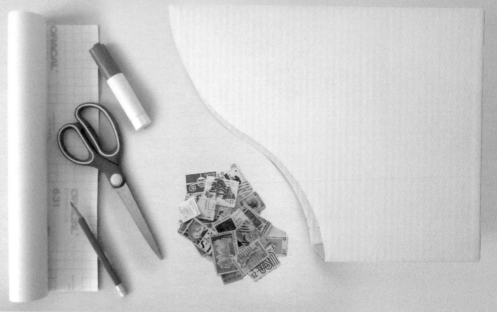

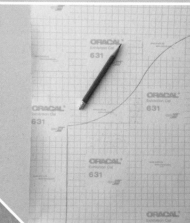

1.
Line up your file box with the bottom right corner of the vinyl paper.

2.
Draw around the file box onto the back of the paper.

3.
Sketch the outline of an elephant (or whatever animal you like) in the center of the file box shape.

4.
Carefully cut out the file box and elephant shapes.

5.
Place the vinyl paper over the file box, lining up the edges. Trace around the elephant onto the file box, then remove the paper. Stick the stamps onto the file box, covering the elephant.

6.
Place the vinyl paper back over the file box, but this time slowly peel away the sticky backing. Smooth the paper down so it sticks to the file box, revealing your stamp-tastic design!

STAMP-IMAL FILE BOX

NELLY THE ELE-STAMP!

STAMP! **STOMP!** **STAMP!**

PAPER BEAD
BRACELET

WEAVE
AND WEAR!

MATERIALS
colored paper (8½ in x 11 in), scissors, ruler, needle, twine

1.
Cut each sheet of paper into ¼-in wide strips. Fold one strip in half widthwise. Use the crease to help you form a point at the center, as shown. Do the same on another strip.

2.
Now weave the two pieces together, as shown, pulling them tightly so the two folded points hook together.

3.
Begin weaving the four strips together as follows:
a. Pull the strip on the far left over the strip to the right of it.
b. Pull the strip on the far right under the strip to the left of it, then over the next strip to the left. Pull taut so the paper curves. Repeat this step six more times, until you have a ball.

a   b

4.
To secure, pull the strip on the far left under a strip on the paper ball (the one closest to it).

left strip

5.
Pull this strip out the other side of the one on the ball, as shown. Trim the strip to align it with the shape of the ball.

6.
Repeat steps 4 and 5 for the other three strips to form a ball; first with the far right strip, then the remaining left strip, then the remaining right strip.

7.
Then repeat steps 1 to 5 until you have enough beads to go around your wrist. Thread the twine through the needle, and slide on the beads. Finish by tying your paper bracelet to your wrist with a double knot!

203

FLOOR
SNAKES
AND
LADDERS

FINISH

36 35 34

25 24 23 22

21 23 22

13 14 15

11 10

1 2 3

START

SNAKE, RATTLE, AND ROLL!

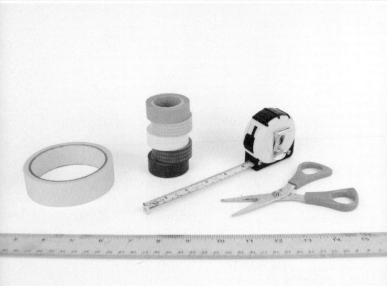

MATERIALS

masking tape,
brown, green, yellow, and red rolls of washi tape,
scissors,
tape measure,
ruler

* Ask an adult for permission before doing this craft.

1. To make a giant-sized version of this popular board game, first create a square (each side 72 in) on the floor with masking tape.

2. Stick another five strips of masking tape (each 72 in long) vertically inside the square, as shown. Leave a gap of 12 in between each strip.

3. Repeat step 2, but this time place the strips horizontally, to form a grid of 36 squares in total. Now you're ready to create the numbers for the board game.

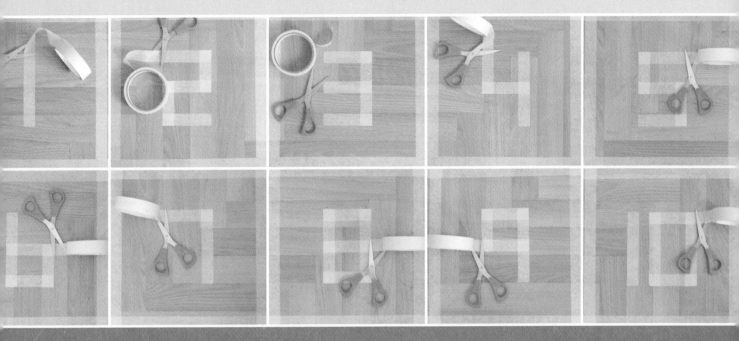

4. Before you make the numbers, note the order, shown on pages 204–205.

5. Now create the numbers with masking tape. Try to keep them roughly the same size for each digit (6 in high and 4 in wide). See the pictures above for help.

6. Place the numbers, one at a time, in the middle of each square as you go. For numbers made up of two digits, leave a gap of ¾ in between each digit.

7. To make a ladder, first cut two strips of brown washi tape, each 24 in long, and place them 4 in apart on the game, as shown.

8. Now cut five 4 in strips of tape and place them across the two longer pieces of tape. Create two more ladders in the same way and position them on the game, as shown on pages 204–205.

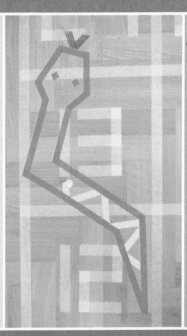

9. Using the green, yellow, and red rolls of washi tape, copy the picture on the left to create three snakes. Position them on the game, as shown on pages 204–205.

HOW TO PLAY
Roll the giant dice from pages 208–209 to move around the game, and use plastic cups for counters. Don't forget to climb up the ladders and slide down the slippery snakes as you go!

MATERIALS

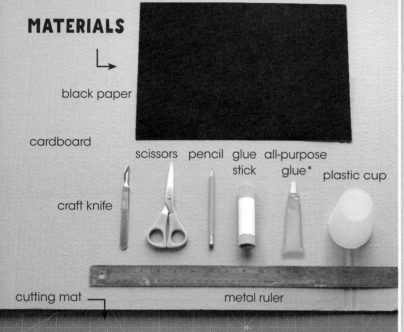

black paper

cardboard

scissors   pencil   glue stick   all-purpose glue*   plastic cup

craft knife

cutting mat   metal ruler

DICE TEMPLATE
(not to size)

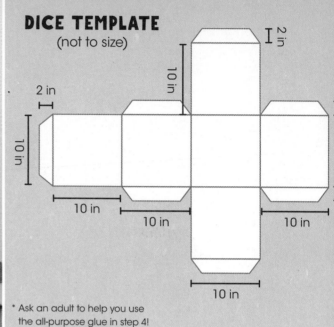

2 in

10 in

2 in

10 in

10 in   10 in   10 in

10 in

* Ask an adult to help you use the all-purpose glue in step 4!

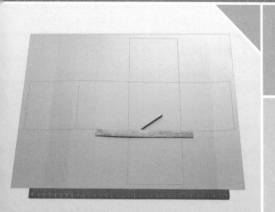

1.
Use a ruler and pencil to copy the dice template onto cardboard.

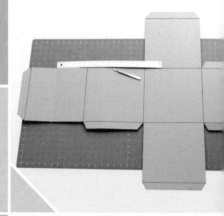

2.
Cut around the outer edge of the template, using the craft knife and ruler on a cutting mat. Now score along the remaining pencil lines.*

* Ask an adult to help with this step.

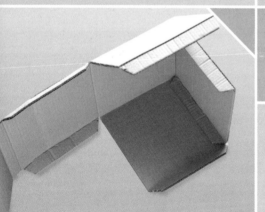

3.
Fold along the scored lines and start bending the cardboard into a cube.

4.
Add all-purpose glue to the tabs, then glue them to the inside of the cube. Hold each tab in place until set.

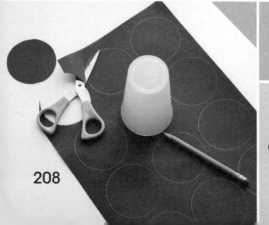

208

5.
Next, draw around the cup onto black paper to create 21 circles. Then cut them all out.

6.
Glue one circle to a side, then six circles to the opposite side. Add two circles to another side, then five circles opposite. Add three circles to another side, then four circles opposite. Now you're ready to play!

GIANT DICE

IT'S DIE-NORMOUS!

HULA
HOOP
RUG

HULA YA CALLING RUGGED?

Hula hoops are great for twirling around your body ... and weaving! Use your favorite giant hoop as the frame loom for this chunky rug craft.

MATERIALS
hula hoop,
old cotton T-shirt,
yarn,
rope (or twine),
pom-poms on thread,
scissors

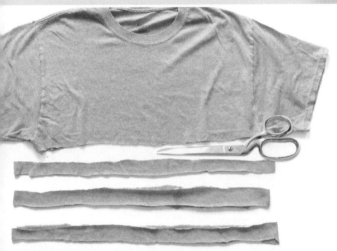

1. Cut the T-shirt horizontally into long strips, stopping just beneath the sleeves (discard the bottom strip with the hem if it's not as stretchy as the rest). You will need at least eight strips.

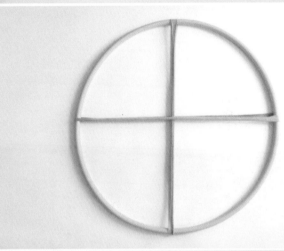

2. Slide and stretch two of the strips across the hula hoop to form a cross, as shown.

3. Continue doing this until you have at least eight strips on the hoop. It should look a little bit like a bicycle wheel.

4. Now you're ready to start weaving the yarn around the spokes. Tie a double knot in the yarn at the center of the rug, as shown.

5. Now weave the yarn in and out of the spokes, pulling it tightly as you go.

6. Keep going around the spokes until you're ready to use another material (different-colored yarn, rope, or pom-poms on thread).

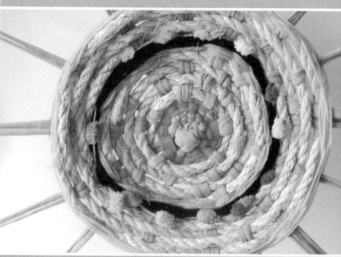

7. When you're ready to switch material, tie one end of the new yarn or material to the end of the yarn already woven into the spokes.

8. Repeat steps 5 to 7, adding either the yarn, rope, or pom-poms, and continue to build up your rug.

9. Keep going until you're happy with the rug's size.

10. To remove the rug from the hoop, cut off the T-shirt spokes, as shown.

11. Continue until all the spokes are free and your rug is no longer attached to the hula hoop.

12. Now tuck the ends of a spoke over and through the last woven row of yarn or material. Then pull it tight, as shown. This is called a lark's head knot.

13. Tie the ends together in a secure double knot. Repeat steps 12 to 13 on the other spokes.

14. Trim the spokes so they are all the same length. These are now the rug's tassels.

15. Add color to the tassels by wrapping different-colored yarn around the top of each one.

16. Tie a double knot in the yarn (around the back). Then your rug is ready to use!

213

MATERIALS

sewing machine (optional),
pencil,
needle,
thread,
glue stick,
colored cardstock x 16
(4 in x 4 in),
buttons x 16,
scissors,
eraser,
white cardstock
(18 in x 18 in)

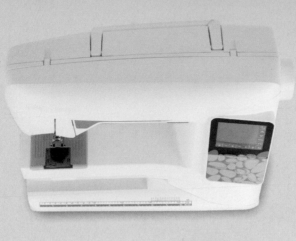 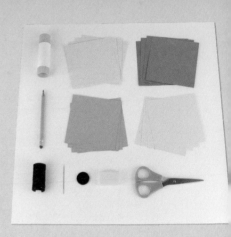

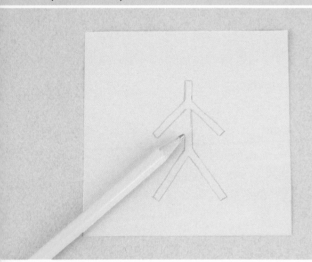

1. Draw a stick person in the middle of a piece of colored cardstock, leaving the head area blank, as shown.

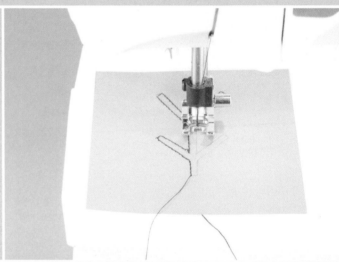

2. Starting at the stick person's neck, use the sewing machine to sew straight lines along the pencil ma Keep the needle in the down position and lift the presser foot to change direction as you go. Contir stitching around the stick person until you return the start, then trim the thread ends.

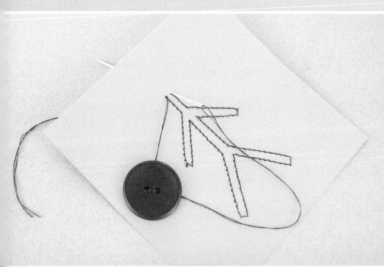

3. Sew a button to the top of the stick person's neck (for the head). Tie a double knot at the back of the cardstock to secure the button head in place.

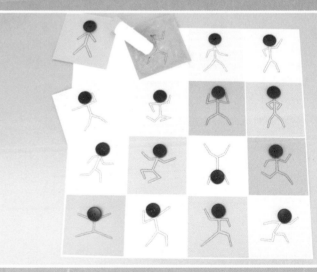

4. Use the eraser to remove any pencil lines. Repeat steps 1 to 3 until you have 16 stick people in different kinds of action poses. Now glue the squares onto the white cardstock and frame your stick-tastic creations!

READY, SET ...
SEW!

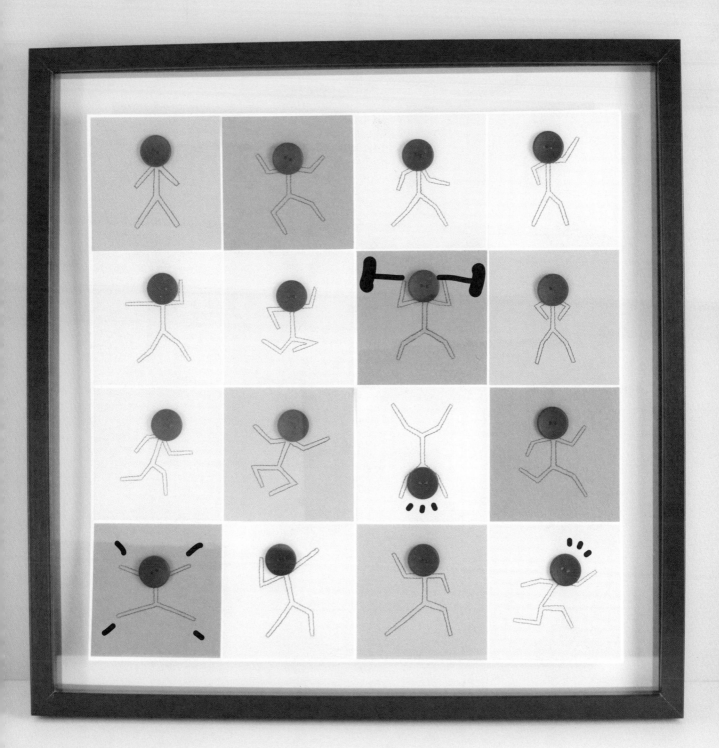

A TUBULAR ADVENT CALENDAR

COUNTDOWN TO CHRISTMAS!